D1177567

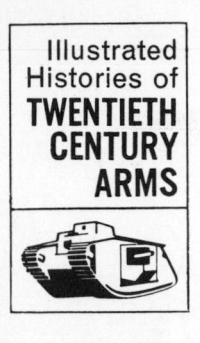

Illustrated
Histories of
**TWENTIETH
CENTURY
ARMS**

ALLIED BAYONETS
OF WORLD WAR II

Other volumes in this series

GERMAN INFANTRY WEAPONS OF WORLD WAR II
by A. J. Barker

BRITISH AND AMERICAN INFANTRY WEAPONS OF
WORLD WAR II by A. J. Barker

TANKS OF WORLD WAR I: BRITISH AND GERMAN
by Peter Chamberlain and Chris Ellis

1. New Zealand infantrymen training in Britain in 1940 with Pattern 1907 bayonet.

ALLIED BAYONETS
OF WORLD WAR II

United Kingdom, United States and U.S.S.R.
India and Australia
France, Belgium and the Netherlands
Denmark and Norway
Poland and Greece

by

J. ANTHONY CARTER

ARCO PUBLISHING COMPANY, INC
New York

Published by
Arco Publishing Company, Inc.
219 Park Avenue South
New York, N. Y. 10003

Library of Congress Catalog Card Number 69–13592
Arco Book Number 668–01862–3

Printed in Great Britain

Contents

		Page
Plate 1. New Zealand Infantrymen with Pattern 1907 bayonet		Frontispiece
Plates 2 and 3. Dissembled bayonets		6

Introduction   7

Allied Bayonets of World War II   11

> United Kingdom
> India
> Australia
> United States
> France
> U.S.S.R.
> Eastern Europe
> Scandinavia
> Belgium

Plates 4–5.	Nomenclature	15–16
Plates 6–8.	Australia	17–20
Plates 9–10.	Belgium	21–23
Plates 11.	Denmark	24
Plates 12–18.	France	25–31
Plates 19–21.	Greece	32–34
Plates 22–25.	India	35–38
Plates 26–30.	Netherlands	39–43
Plates 31–34.	Norway	44–47
Plates 35–36.	Poland	48–49
Plates 37–46.	United Kingdom	50–59
Plates 47–55.	United States	60–67
Plates 56–66.	U.S.S.R.	69–75

Appendices:

1. Comparative Lengths of Allied Bayonets	76–77
2. Captured Bayonets	78
3. Collecting Bayonets	79–80

Select Bibliography   80

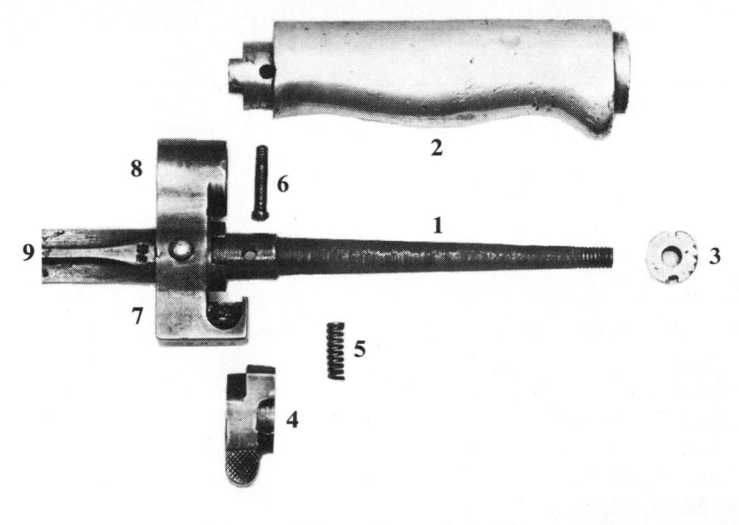

2. The French Model 1866/93/16 dismantled. The numbered parts are identified as follows: 1. Blade tang. 2. Brass hilt. 3. Hilt securing nut. 4. Rotating press stud mechanism. 5. Press stud spring. 6. Hilt base screw, which also regulates movement of press stud. 7. Crossguard. 8. Muzzle ring. 9. Cruciform blade.

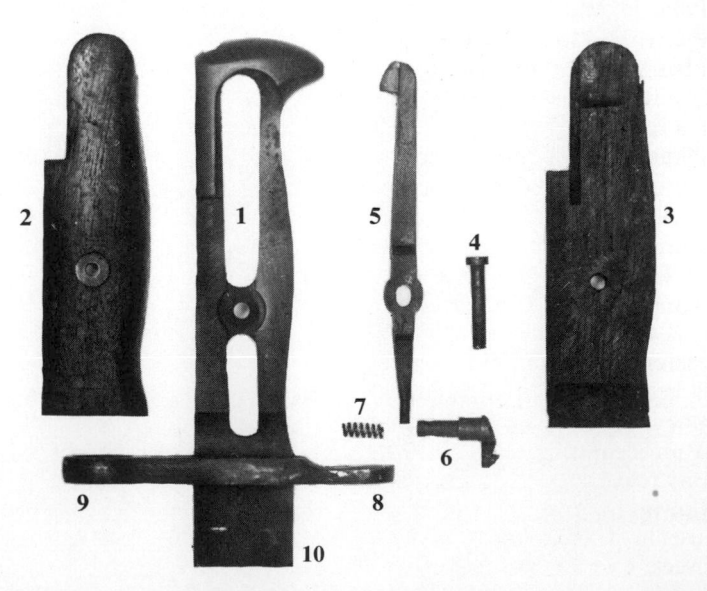

3. The U.S.A. Model 1905 dismantled. The numbered parts are identified as follows: 1. Blade tang and pommel. 2. Wood grip. 3. Wood grip —inside view. 4. Grips retaining bolt and pivot for catch. 5. Pivoting catch, which slots into hole in press stud. 6. Press stud with scabbard mouthpiece catch. 7. Press stud spring. 8. Cross guard with straight quillon. 9. Muzzle ring. 10. Blade.

INTRODUCTION

This volume illustrates and describes the principal bayonets used by the Allied armies throughout World War II. Some nations completely rearmed between the wars, while others retained infantry weapons first issued during the 19th century. However, all bayonets issued to the armed forces fighting Germany, Italy and Japan between 1939 and 1946 are included. In *Allied Bayonets of World War II* are studied not only the bayonets of the great powers Britain and the United States, together with the Soviet Union, but also other combatant nations such as India and Australia, France, Belgium and the Netherlands, Norway, Denmark, Poland and Greece. In spite of the fact that this of all weapons has the most rudimentary and obvious task to perform no other arm has been altered and replaced by new models as has the bayonet this century. It is simply a blade to convert a rifle to a stabbing weapon. In the last few years most countries have adopted a short knife bayonet, whether single edged, double edged, bowie bladed, detachable or attached or folding. All these types are at present in service throughout the world. Very few armies have been equipped with a bayonet that was only a bayonet. Too often the efficiency of one arm has been sacrificed to the need for a secondary arm, whether knife, machete or sword.

Thus in the pages of this book dealing in a specialised period there can be found bayonets with all the blades mentioned above as well as those with round blades, long and short cruciform blades, blades with the cutting edge facing downwards and upwards and slim T-backed blades. When the perfect bayonet is produced it will differ little from those used now or in the past: every possibility seems to have been tried, never to everyone's satisfaction. I hope therefore that the many and varying designs shown in this book will be as fascinating and absorbing to the reader as they have been to me in its compilation.

I am deeply grateful to those who have given me so much help in my researches and I should like to express my appreciation to the following: Dr. C. H. Roads and the staff of the Imperial War Museum, London; Mr. F. Askgaard, Chief Curator of the Tøjhusmuseet, Copenhagen; Colonel Jacques Wemaere of the Musée de l'Armée, Paris; Captain A. Gundeid of the Haermuseet, Oslo;

Mr. K. C. B. Gorlitz of the Nederlands Leger en Wapenmuseum "General Hoefer", Leiden.

I must thank especially R. J. Wilkinson-Latham not only for his encouragement but also for his valued advice; Dr. James A. Maddox, Lieutenant, U.S.N., D.C., for his assistance and hard work in finding many rare specimens for me; Major a.D. Hans Rudolf von Stein, whose long and detailed study of the subject has proved invaluable and who has provided the answers to many problems; Guy Vaermans for his hospitality and help in the research for uncatalogued models; Kevin Bestt for lending me some of the rarer bayonets from his excellent collection.

Other collectors and dealers have given their time and help to me. I do them an injustice to list them below; but they all have my gratitude, for without any one of them there would be a gap in this volume: Ray Allen, Roger Cleverly, Adrian Dagger, Roger Evans, Tom Greenaway, George Kellam, Dr. John Kennaugh, Claude Meunier, David Jeffcoat.

I am grateful to the collectors and museums mentioned below, without whose valuable co-operation the following plates could not have been reproduced: 16, 26, Imperial War Museum, London; 17, 18, 42, 55, Kevin Bestt; 28, Nederlands Leger en Wapenmuseum, Leiden; 30, 31, 32, Haermuseet, Oslo; 48, Dr. John Kennaugh; 56, 62, 63, David Jeffcoat.

Finally a word of special thanks is owed to Miss Caroline Bonsor for her encouragement while preparing this volume.

Allied Bayonets of World War II

In their 300 years' history bayonets have seen many changes as the nature of armed conflict has altered. While the weapon's actual value in causing damage to or killing an enemy has sometimes been in dispute the naked blade of the fixed bayonet is always of undoubted psychological comfort to the infantryman when the enemy is in sight. In World War II the bayonet was of special value in military action such as night patrols, jungle warfare and street fighting, and in stubborn defensive actions of which the Battle for Stalingrad is a classic example. It has also been shown to be the ideal weapon for controlling unarmed people, whether they are prisoners or civilians in occupied countries.

In this book are the bayonets of all the nations which fought between 1939 and 1946 against Germany, Italy and Japan. For some the war was short and the bayonets they used were unchanged from the days of World War I or even earlier. Some nations gave little or no thought to the development of the weapon following the lessons learned after 1918 but every nation has its own views, based largely on the battle conditions it expects its soldiers to encounter, as to the most effective bayonet. For Great Britain and the United States World War II saw the change from the sword bayonet in use during the 19th century and World War I to the short-bladed spike or knife bayonet. The British World War I bayonets had a blade length of 17in, but for World War II they were shortened to just under 8in. The United States Model 1905 used in World War I had a 16in blade, but this shortened to 10in and, eventually, to under 7in. Russian bayonets dropped by just under 5in in length.

The arguments for the change to knife bayonet were expounded at length, based on the lessons learned from World War I, by a report from the British Small Arms School published in 1924. The long World War I bayonets were criticised as follows:—"In the war the utility of the bayonet as a cutlass or dagger proved to be negligible, hence the demand for trench knives, clubs, etc. As a means of clearing brushwood, etc. it is one of the most futile instruments imaginable. Even for cutting up duckboards and ammunition boxes for firewood it was ineffective, and it generally suffered severely in the contest. As a poker it was excellent, but this will apply to any form of bayonet. The handle form necessitated a two-

9

point method of attachment to the rifle: thus a heavy nose-cap was required, which further increased the unhandiness of the rifle for bayonet fighting and shooting—particularly snapshooting. The difference in average scoring capability is estimated as being 10 to 20% lower in the case of troops who fire with the bayonets fixed. It is not so much the amount that the bayonet affects the actual shooting of the rifle that matters, as the great unhandiness in snap-shooting and rapid fire, and the additional surface exposed to wind pressure in gusty winds. The long broad blade glints even in moonlight and when Very lights are fired. As a killing shape it makes a very nasty wound, but is of bad section for penetration and worse for withdrawal. Owing to its great length and the leverage exerted it frequently breaks or bends, even against straw-filled sacks and in spite of being kept properly sharpened."

United Kingdom

Great Britain had been armed throughout World War I with the Pattern 1907 sword bayonet, which in 1924 was redesignated the No 1 Mk 1. This weapon had a single-edged blade 17in long, and it became the most widely used bayonet in history. Its production during the two World Wars approached four million. During the First World War and in the 1920s considerable research was made into the development of a replacement weapon. The 1924 Small Arms School report, quoted above, stated:

"It has been conclusively proved during the war, and since, with our present system of training in the bayonet, that 'reach' is not the main factor but that 'handiness' is. A man with a short handy weapon will beat an equally skilled man with a long cumbersome weapon practically every time. As regards length of blade for killing purposes, the Physical Training Staff went into this in considerable detail during the war, and came to the conclusion that a 6in blade was sufficiently long to deal with the most thickly clad of our enemies—potential or otherwise." The most thickly clad enemy was taken as being a Russian in winter clothing.

Following this report, which included further detail on the projected new weapon, tests led to the eventual official adoption in November 1939 of the No 4 Mk 1 spike bayonet. Its cruciform blade, also favoured by the Russians, was replaced by a round spike during the war for economic reasons. In September 1944 a short bowie bladed knife bayonet was introduced for use on the Jungle Carbine. This return to a dual purpose weapon was influenced by American experience in the Pacific, where they had introduced a

10

short bayonet based on their fighting knife in an area where close combat was more usual than in Europe.

Canada, New Zealand, Rhodesia and South Africa armed themselves with British arms.

India

India's supply of arms was inadequate to meet the demand of the war against Japan and many rifle and bayonet components were shipped to India to be completed by their factories. Trials to find a cheap solution to their preference for a shorter bayonet for Jungle warfare had led them to cut down some Pattern 1907s to a length of 12in in 1941, and these were redesignated the Mk I*. Few of these were manufactured as supplies of hilt parts and scabbards from Britain prompted them to manufacture a 12in blade without fullers to fit the hilts from 1942–45. In the latter years of the war many were issued with unfinished hilts and the scabbards were not shortened until after the war.

Australia

Australia looked for a more suitable weapon for use in the jungles and their experiments were along the same lines as other countries. It resulted in the Owen sub-machine gun bayonet, which was simply a Pattern 1907 with a short blade, better suited for knife fighting than its longer parent. A more unusual weapon, the experimental machete bayonet, is included in this book because while it was experimental production started and over 2,000 were made. The machete bayonet took its design from the U.S. army machete and it was hoped would be an ideal arm in the jungle, combining the qualities of knife, bayonet and machete. However, its excessive weight and poor balance proved its impracticability.

United States

The United States entered the war armed with their Model 1905 Springfield bayonet and a modification of this, the M 1942. The latter had plastic grips to combat wood rot in the Pacific. The Americans were quick to act on suggestions, made by the U.S. Cavalry Board in late 1942, that a shorter bayonet would be more suitable for men on horseback and for troops travelling and lurching about in the back of transports. The same points in favour of a shorter bayonet that faced the British were considered and the M 42s in production and those already produced were shortened, and furthermore a new model was put into production similar to the shortened model, but was manufactured with a new blade. These

11

were the M 1 models used on the M 1 Garand Rifle throughout the war. They were equipped with green plastic scabbards that were easily cleaned, rustfree, rot proof and quieter when carried at the side or when a bayonet was carefully withdrawn.

While these M 1 shortened bayonets were an improvement on the earlier patterns the Headquarters, Army Service Forces, were not satisfied and expressed their desire for a new bayonet for the M 1 Carbine based more on the U.S. army fighting knife. U.S. forces had carried the fighting knife, the M 3, as well as a bayonet. Obviously one dual-purpose weapon was preferable and the final model approved for adoption by the Infantry Board in January 1944 was an M 3 knife with a new crossguard. This incorporated a muzzle ring and a modified pommel with two sprung catches enabling it to be attached firmly to the carbine. In all other respects the bayonet was an exact copy of the efficient fighting knife with a short double-edged blade and a well contoured and corrugated hilt. In spite of the changeover to plastic grips on other models the hilt of this bayonet was made of leather rings compressed together, which was extremely prone to damage from mildew and fungus. Not until 1956, well after the war was over, were the leather grips replaced by two-piece plastic grips. The scabbards were, however, plastic from the first.

The United States had in 1943 discarded all their previous findings to adopt the Johnson Dagger Bayonet for the Johnson Semi-Automatic Rifle Model 1941. This crudely-made and -designed arm has little to recommend it in comparison with the U.S. knife bayonets. It is a weapon designed by Captain Johnson merely as a last-ditch defensive weapon. An unpopular and poor weapon, its design was partly dictated by the rifle, whose recoiling barrel ruled out any but the lightest bayonet. Consequently it cannot really be considered as a stage in the development of the U.S. bayonet: rather a specialised excursion.

France

France did little to improve or redesign her bayonets between the wars. Following other European countries' practice, in 1935 the Lebel bayonets, first issued in 1886, were shortened, but this directive was ignored by most elements in the French army and by all the colonial troops. The long thin cruciform blade of this bayonet and its variations continued, in spite of its proneness to bending and snapping after a thrust, as the principal infantry bayonet of the French troops. It was a complicated and expensive weapon to produce and virtually useless as anything but a thrusting arm. The

Model 1892 bayonet still in use was a better weapon and could be used as a knife for thrusting and cutting as well as a good general purpose tool. Its blade length of 15¾in was comparatively long for World War II. Plastic grips and shortened quillons officially cut down in 1915 were slight improvements though production of full quillons continued.

The only major French innovation was their adoption of the rod bayonet on the M.A.S. Model 1936 Rifle. This slim round rod bayonet was carried reversed in the stock below the barrel and could be withdrawn and locked into position by lugs on the rod. An interesting weapon but one lacking strength and useful solely as a thrusting arm. The United States had issued and experimented for years with rod bayonets only to abandon them long before the French adoption of this type of weapon. In general France preferred to stay with her large assortment of well tried weapons from the First War and overlooked their faults.

U.S.S.R.

The Soviet Union followed their practice of ignoring all that everyone else found preferable so that their history of bayonet design is based on premises completely independent in theory and design. Russia had based her military strategy on massed formations, which concentrated on overwhelming an enemy rather than defeating him by the skill of the individual soldier. Consequently accuracy was sacrificed for mass fire power and the bayonet's effect on accuracy was ignored by all but their snipers. Their standard infantry bayonet was a cruciform bladed socket bayonet and the type used in the World War II was first adopted in 1891 and modified slightly between the wars. This bayonet, while it was detachable, was intended to be carried fixed at all times and used purely as a thrusting weapon in close combat, never as a sword or dagger. The Russians therefore issued no scabbards with these bayonets and those found in scabbards are weapons captured by the Austrians or Germans during the 1914–18 War. To all but the Soviets this type of bayonet had passed with the 19th century.

In 1936 Russia adopted its first knife bayonet, a single-edged cutting and thrusting weapon, for use on the M 1936 Simnov automatic rifle. Automatic fire made the bayonet less important as a permanent fixture and interfered with the rifle's performance. Consequently Russia began to develop knife bayonets for their Automatic rifles and in 1938 and 1940 new models were designed for the Tokarevs. These are well made and well balanced dual purpose weapons and served the Soviet troops well in close combat

13

with the Germans in Stalingrad. On their conventional rifles, however, the Soviets continued their earlier practice and as late as 1944 a form of socket bayonet that would fold alongside the stock was issued with the last Mosin–Nagant Carbine Model 1944. Russia continued to the end of the war to regard the bayonet as an extra with secondary purposes only on their automatic weapons, believing that huge massed formations with rifles and bayonet fixed could swamp an enemy whatever the casualties.

Eastern Europe

Little of importance in the advancement or otherwise of bayonet design was attempted by the other countries which fought with the Allies in the 1939–45 War. Most Eastern European countries and the Baltic states fell under Germany and Austria's sphere of influence in arms design. The majority had armed themselves by buying export arms from Germany and Austria; consequently short single-edged knife bayonets were in use by the Poles, which were very similar to the German infantry bayonet and interchangeable on Polish and German Mausers.

Scandinavia

The Scandinavian countries retained unaltered bayonets that were first issued in the 1890s. Norway's M 1894 with éither long or short blade was used throughout the war. Its single-edged blade had an unusual feature, the pivoted bar press which was copied early in the century by the United States on their M 1905 Springfield bayonet. All U.S. bayonets up to the M 4 utilised this catch, so the Norwegian bayonet had a lasting effect on U.S. practice. Denmark retained their M 1915 T-backed slim sword bayonet: a design used by the Dutch on their M 1895 bayonets, though some were issued with short double-edged blades.

Belgium

Belgium, after World War I, took over from Mausers the production of F.N.-made Mausers, which were exported all over the world, especially to South America. In consequence of their boom in arms sales some effort sas made to produce a better infantry bayonet, and weapons of four different lengths were produced for export. In 1916 and 1924 Belgium had produced for themselves bayonets with long, slim double-edged blades, better suited to thrusting than cutting, but much sturdier than the French thrusting bayonets.

14

BRITISH PATTERN 1907 SWORD BAYONET AND SCABBARD

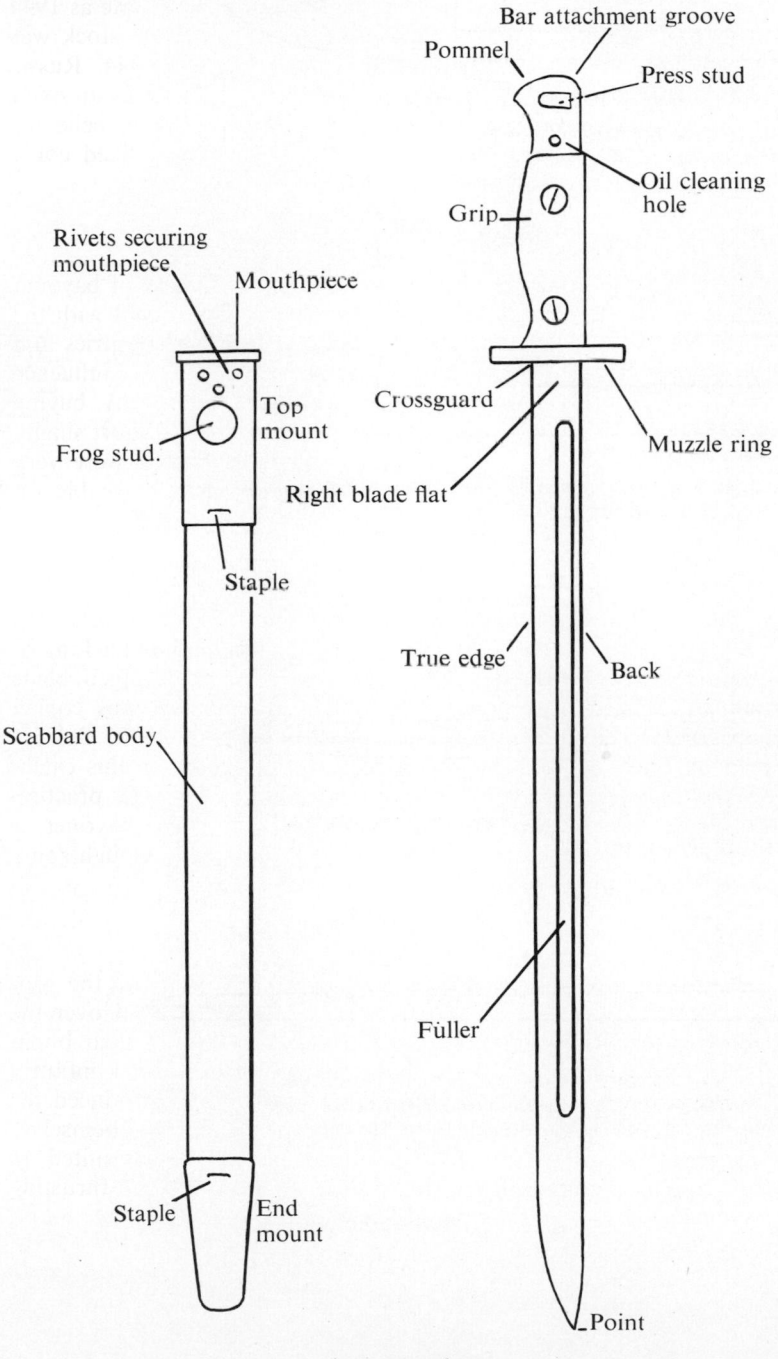

4. *Nomenclature*

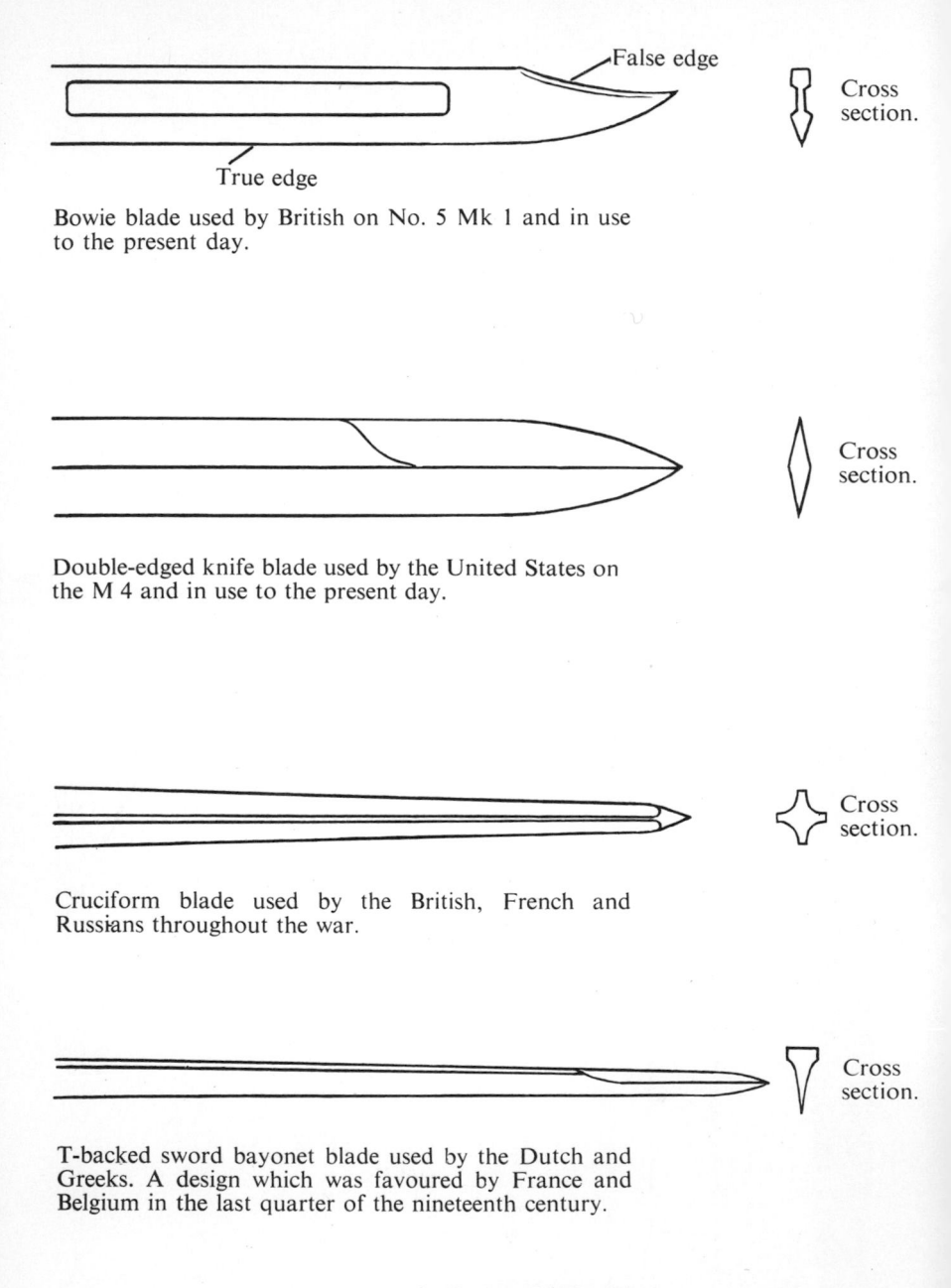

False edge

Cross section.

True edge

Bowie blade used by British on No. 5 Mk 1 and in use to the present day.

Cross section.

Double-edged knife blade used by the United States on the M 4 and in use to the present day.

Cross section.

Cruciform blade used by the British, French and Russians throughout the war.

Cross section.

T-backed sword bayonet blade used by the Dutch and Greeks. A design which was favoured by France and Belgium in the last quarter of the nineteenth century.

5. *Bayonet blades*

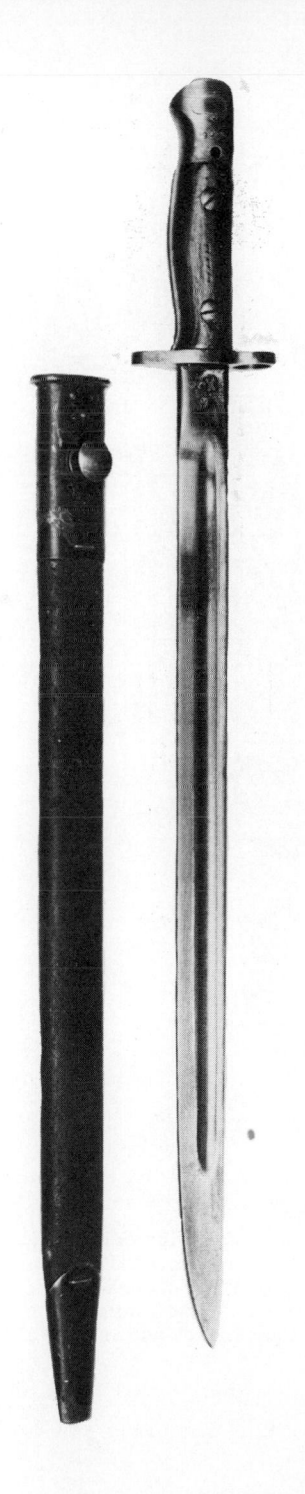

6. *Pattern 1907 Sword Bayonet*

This bayonet is exactly the same model as that used by the British forces except that it was manufactured in Australia and was issued throughout the war. Australia never adopted the No 4 rifle so consequently did not utilise the No. 4 spike bayonets. This Pattern 1907 was therefore their standard infantry bayonet.

The blade finish is different from that found on British made bayonets as the heavily blued blade is highly polished. The leather scabbard body is left brown, although the steel mounts are lightly blued. In all other respects save the markings it is identical to the British model.

The grips are stamped SLAZ 42, showing that these were produced separately by the firm of Slazenger in 1942. The pommel has the serial number C 90287. The left blade flat is marked MA 1907 and with the date of manufacture 11 42 for November 1942. The right flat has the War Department broad arrow over OA beside the two crossed lines. The top scabbard mount is stamped MA.

Blade length: 17in
Overall length: 21¾in
Muzzle ring diameter: 17mm
Weight: 18oz
Rifle: S.M.L.E.

17

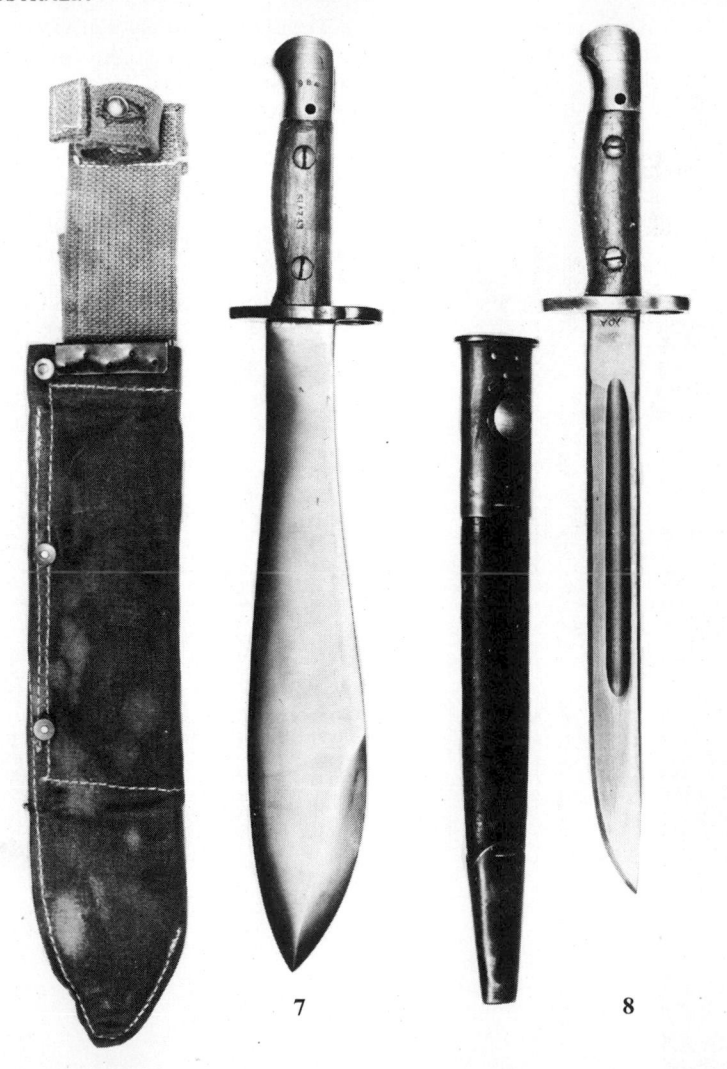

7   8

7. *Pattern 1943 Machete Bayonet—Experimentally Issued*

While Australian forces were fighting the Japanese in the Pacific the military authorities designed a weapon which was intended to perform the duties of a bayonet and a jungle machete. The blade form was that of the American bolo knife and on paper the design seemed suitable for jungle warfare. The United States had issued their troops with machete

18

or bolo bayonets at the beginning of the century after their experiences in the Spanish–American War and in the Philippines, but had abandoned these arms after finding that a dual-purpose bayonet of this design proved inadequate in either role.

The same problems arose with this bayonet which was issued experimentally in small numbers and soon abandoned in favour of more conventional weapons.

The hilt is of the same pattern as that used on the P 1907, but the blade, made without fullers, swells out into a broad machete, which was extremely clumsy when used as a thrusting weapon. The back of the blade along the spear-shaped point was sharpened to form a double edge. Although the blade swells past the line of the muzzle ring this did not effect firing since it was attached to the boss below the barrel of the S.M.L.F. rifle. The blade and metal parts of the hilt are heavily blued.

The green canvas scabbard is stitched and reinforced by copper rivets with a blued steel mouthpiece and steel reinforcement sewn inside the scabbard point. A webbing frog with loop is stitched to the back of the body.

The grips are stamped SLAZ 43 for Slazenger 1943 and the pommel is stamped with the serial number 3984. The right blade flat has a War Department broad arrow. The scabbard is marked R.M.B. Ltd. 1943 on the back.

Blade length: 11⅜in
Overall length: 16in
Muzzle ring diameter: 17mm
Rifle: S.M.L.E.

8. *Model 1943 Knife Bayonet*

This short knife bayonet, used only by the Australians, was designed for their Owen sub-machine gun and is basically a shortened Pattern 1907 except that the blade was manufactured as a knife blade and was not cut down from a longer P 07 bayonet.

It is an extremely well made and well balanced weapon. The hilt retains all the details of the P 07. All metal parts including the scabbard mounts are heavily blued.

The scabbard is the same as that used with the P 07 except that the body is shorter and the tip of the steel end mount is flat.

The only markings on the hilt are on the grips which are stamped SLAZ 43 to show that they were made by the firm of Slazenger in 1943. One concludes these grips were made earlier than this particular bayonet, as it is stamped on the left side of the blade 11 44 for November 1944 under MA over 1907, and this shows its close relationship to the basic design, which is still that of the P 07. On the right side of the blade is the Australian Ordnance mark OA under a War Department broad arrow.

Blade length: 10⅛in
Overall length: 14·9in
Muzzle ring diameter: 17mm
Weight: 12oz
Owen 9mm Pattern 1943 Sub-machine Gun (Machine Carbine)

Jungle Carbine Bayonet Pattern 1944

The Australian forces fighting in the Pacific first requested a light rifle or carbine for jungle warfare in 1942. However, at that date their total arms production was working to capacity manufacturing the S.M.L.E., the Bren and the Vickers machine gun. Some experiments were made with a lightened S.M.L.E. which failed to meet the requirements. Eventually in 1944 a copy of the British No. 5 Jungle Carbine with a few modifications was the final model to be tried. This carbine was accepted for the Australian Army but was not produced in quantity. The war was in its final stages at the time of the carbine's adoption and though first requested in 1942 it was produced too late to be issued on anything but an experimental scale.

While the Australians accepted the majority of features of the carbine the British No 5 Mk I bayonet was rejected in favour of a modified Pattern 1907. The bayonet issued was identical to the Australian Pattern 1907 in everything except the crossguard. This enabled them to produce the bayonet more quickly than retooling for a completely new design. The crossguard was modified to give it a much larger muzzle ring to fit over the carbine's flash eliminator. The lower part of the guard had a hole drilled through it similar to the British bayonet. In all other respects it is identical to the Pattern 1907 including the T-shaped pommel groove. This is because the Australian copy of the carbine did not use the round bayonet lug that is a feature of the British carbine.

Markings found on these bayonets show that the grips were made by Slazengers in 1944. The blades have the Australian ordnance mark OA under the broad arrow. They are stamped with the date of manufacture in early 1945.

An example has been examined which has had the blade shortened and modified to the pattern used on the British No 5 bayonet. It has been cut down and reground to a bowie blade 7·8in long. This modification was made to a few bayonets experimentally after the war.

Blade length: 17in
Overall length: 21¾in
Muzzle ring diameter: 23mm
Weight: 18oz
Rifle: Australian copy of British No 5 Mk I Jungle Carbine.
  Experimentally issued

9

10

21

9. *Model 1916 Bayonet*

In 1916 Belgium adopted a new bayonet for their Model 1889 Mauser rifle which would in time replace the original weapons with their assortment of blade lengths. This new bayonet with its tapering double edged blade gave the Belgians a weapon equal in length to those arms carried by the French, British, Russian and German troops.

Though designed with a long tapering blade, it was essentially a thrusting weapon only. A strong central rib runs to the point on both sides of the blade giving it great strength and rigidity. The roughly-ground concave cutting edges have no real edge to them but the cross-section presents an ideal penetrating shape. The metal parts are blued to prevent any reflection from flares. The hilt is conventional in design and has no crossguard quillon in keeping with general practice at this time. One typical Belgian design point is evident in the grip-retaining screws which screw into large round bolt heads. The screw heads cut to take a two pronged tool are set in washers.

The rifle barrel is enclosed in a steel jacket from which only the muzzle protrudes, and the bayonet's muzzle ring is made to fit over the barrel jacket rather than over the muzzle.

The overall finish is poor in that machine and welding marks are clearly visible on both blade and hilt but this does not detract in any way from its strength or serviceability.

The only markings are a small H in a circle on blade, hilt and scabbard and the regimental marking 5935 G.Ie on crossguard and frog stud.

This bayonet together with its modification the Model 1924 saw considerable use during the World War II in the days of bitter fighting before the fall of Belgium on 28th May 1940.

Blade length: 17⅝in
Overall length: 22¾in
Muzzle ring diameter: 17·5mm
Weight: 15oz
Rifle: 7·65mm Model 1889 Mauser Rifle

10. *Model 1924 Bayonet*

In 1924 the Fabrique Nationale factory produced their variation of the German Kar 98 in 7·65mm calibre. This Belgian made Mauser carbine and its variants the M 1924/30 and M 1930 saw service during the fighting in 1940.

The Model 1924 bayonet is identical to the Model 1916 infantry bayonet except that it has a smaller muzzle ring to fit over the the barrel of the Model 1924 Rifle. The scabbard is slightly modified in that the blade retaining springs are held in place by two rivets instead of screws.

A serial number 41956 is on the frog stud and a small H in a circle appears on the crossguard, pommel and press stud. All metal parts are very heavily blued.

Muzzle ring diameter: 15·5mm

22

Model 1924 Bayonet. Shortened

Between the wars a few of the Model 1924 bayonets and scabbards were shortened. As not many were altered it is believed that this modification was only performed experimentally and that a general shortening of bayonets in service was never officially sanctioned.

Those altered have a blade length of 13·18in The original scabbard has been shortened by removing the top with mouthpiece and frog stud and cutting away several inches of the body. The top part has then been reattached to the shortened body so that it overlaps. The scabbard after shortening is 14·17in long.

Model 1916 Gendarmerie Bayonet

Though this bayonet is not strictly a military arm the Belgian Gendarmerie resisted the German invasion alongside regular troops. It is similar to the Model 1916 infantry bayonet in all dimensions except for the shape of the blade. This is T backed similar to the Dutch Model 1895 bayonets. The Belgians had always favoured giving their different branches of the armed forces different bayonets. In 1882 the Gendarmerie had been issued with a long T backed model whose blade was identical to that of the French Model 1874 Gras bayonet. Consequently in 1916 the Gendarmerie retained their blade design though of a shorter length to match the infantry bayonet. It was heavily blued overall. It remained in service during the war.

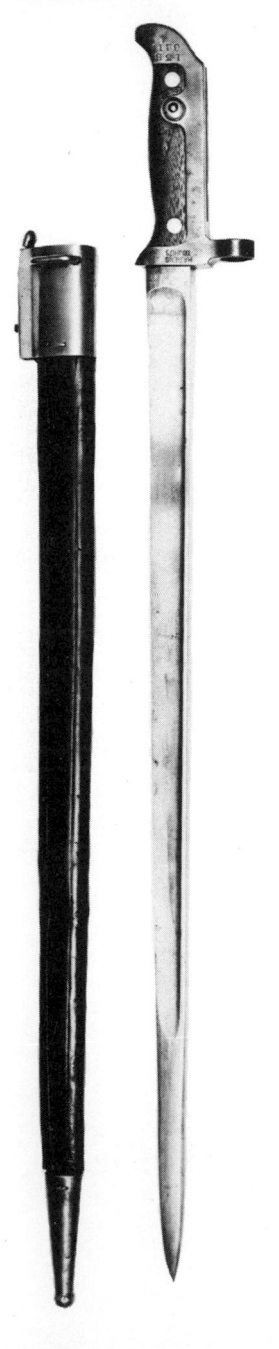

11. *Model 1915 Bayonet*

From 1939 until the Danish armed forces were disbanded by the Germans in 1943 the only bayonet in issue was the Model 1915. The short knife bayonet Model 1889 was found to be inadequate during the 1914–18 War and Denmark therefore in 1915 adopted a new longer bayonet with a slim T-backed blade which between the wars gradually replaced the knife bayonet by 1939. Most other nations involved in World War II were developing and adopting knife bayonets to replace their long sword bayonets.

The slender blade of the Model 1915 has an extremely strong back and a single cutting edge which tapers to a narrow point ideal for thrusting. The small slender hilt is a little too short for a good hand grip. It has no real crossguard, although the lower part protrudes slightly so that a catch on the scabbard clips over it and holds the bayonet firmly and quietly in the scabbard. The pronounced beaked pommel helps the grip but this is not helped by the smooth wood grips held by brass rivets and the coiled spring press stud which is placed a third of the way down the hilt to operate in the long T shaped rifle attachment bar groove.

The steel-mounted leather scabbard is because of its shape very prone to damage from buckling. While the blade was left polished bright the steel hilt and scabbard mounts were blued.

The majority of these bayonets are stamped with a crowned H.V. for the Haerens Vabenarsenal (1923–43) on the crossguard. Others are found stamped in full with the other manufacturers, Haerens Tøjhus (1915–22) and Haerens Rustkammer (1922–32). Each bayonet was also stamped with a fabrication number.

When the Danish army was re-equipped after World War II the M 1915 was abandoned so that it officially ended its life in 1943.

Blade length: 17⅞in
Overall length: 22·08in
Muzzle ring diameter: 14mm
Rifle: 8mm Model 1889–10 Krag-Jorgensen

12. French Croix de Guerre holder with Model 1936 MAS rifle and bayonet in fixed position.

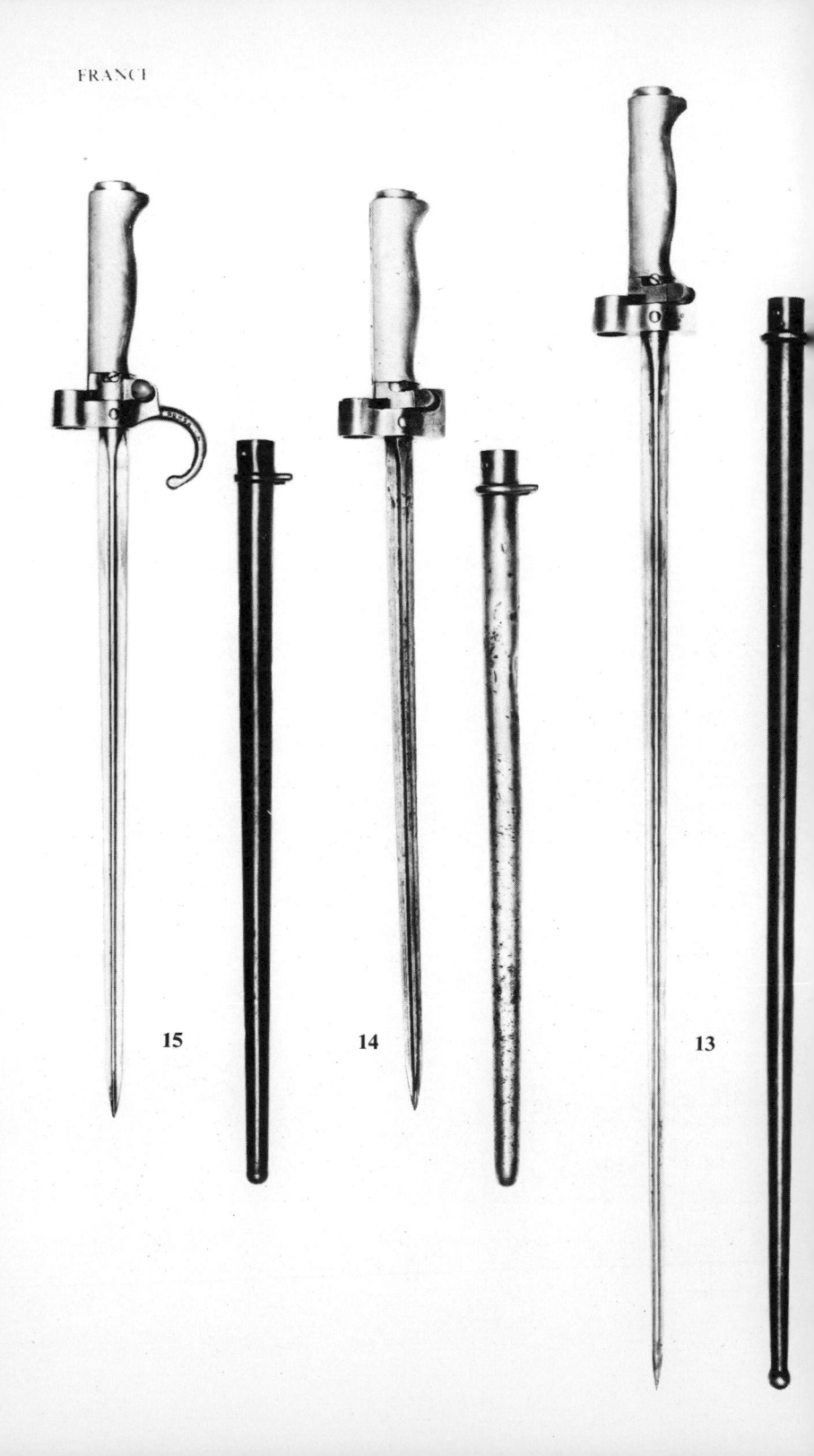

15 14 13

13. *Model 1886/93/16 Epée Bayonet*

The designation of this bayonet, which in this version was manufactured during and after 1916, means that the original pattern was issued in 1886, modified in 1893 and altered again to produce this model, which became France's standard infantry bayonet throughout the 1939–45 war. Many colonial troops continued to carry the earlier patterns, but the regular French army regiments were equipped with the 1916 model, which has two features which distinguish it from its earlier patterns. These are the crossguard, which ends in a rectangular flat without a quillon and the press stud, which is flat and on the same level as the pivoting body of the catch. The part which is pressed is chequered to make for a firm grip.

The long slender cruciform blade was designed purely for thrusting and this was its greatest fault, in that its length and rigidity left it prone to breaking and bending after a thrust. For the same reason the slender tubular scabbards, which were heavily blued, are often found bent or damaged. There is no attachment groove as found on other bayonets, but there is a guide slot along the back of the hilt, which rests along a bar on the barrel. This bar, notched for the press stud, also passes into the base of the muzzle ring, which in turn is cut to enclose the rifle front sight.

The detachable hollow brass hilt through which the blade tang passes to the round nut in the pommel was used on most of these bayonets, although some were equipped with the older white metal hilts and a few with the rarer steel hilts.

There are no distinguishing marks on the bayonet although every part is stamped with French proof and inspection marks.

Blade length: 20½in
Overall length: 25¼in
Muzzle ring diameter: 22mm
Rifles: Model 1886 Lebel 8mm, Model 1886/93 Lebel, Model 1907–15 8mm, Model 1907–15/34 7·5mm, Model 1917 8mm Automatic, Model 1918 8mm Automatic
Variations: Brass hilt, white metal hilt, steel hilt.

14. *Model 1886/93/16/35 Epée Bayonet*

This particular bayonet was modified in 1935 as was the previous model described. The alterations were carried out on all types of the Model 1886 and this model is the last development made originally during or after 1916. More of this model were altered than any other type. The hilt details are as described for the long original bayonet which was still widely used during the short war leading up to France's collapse in 1940.

As the hilt was detachable this type of bayonet can be found with either brass or white metal grip and occasionally with the rare steel grip.

The scabbard has been shortened in a different manner by removing the extra length and then by folding in the cross cut end and brazing the edges together. This was then heavily blued, although the bayonet itself was left finished bright.

Blade length: 13¼in
Overall length: 17⅞in
Muzzle ring diameter: 22mm
Weight: 14oz
Rifles: as for **13.**

15. *Model 1886/35 Epée Bayonet*

In 1935 in keeping with developments by other European countries the French shortened many of their Épée bayonets to form more modern knife bayonets. Officially the length decreed was 33cm (13in), but the lengths of these altered models can vary from 12½ to 13½in. The original bayonet with its long cruciform blade is ideally suited to modifying in this manner since it loses none of its advantages except reach, and gains in strength since the longer bayonet was so prone to bending and breaking.

The scabbards were also shortened by removing the ferrule, cutting away the excess length and then rewelding the round ferrule in position. The finished bayonet was a much improved weapon and could be used as a fighting knife, although only for thrusting. As it has no cutting edges a 9 or 10in blade would have been a better choice for a combined bayonet and fighting knife.

There are two types of this bayonet but the difference is only in the method of securing the handgrip to the blade tang. The first Model 1886 bayonets produced had the tang flattened so that the grip was held permanently in place. All later models were fitted with a round nut which screws onto the threaded tang and rests in a round recess in the flat circular end of the pommel.

This particular model with its white metal hilt has all metal surfaces, including the blade finished bright, although the scabbard is heavily blued.

Blade length: 13in
Overall length: 17⅝in
Weight: 16oz
Muzzle ring diameter: 22mm
Rifles: Model 1886 Lebel 8mm, Model 1886/93 Lebel,
      Model 1907–15 8mm, Model 1907--15/34 7·5mm,
      Model 1917 8mm Automatic, Model 1918 8mm Automatic
Variation: Brass grip on model with detachable hilt.

16. *Model 1892 Knife Bayonet—modified*

The model illustrated has modifications which were made to the bayonet during the 1914–18 war. It saw service with the French armies up to the time of the collapse of France in 1940 and continued to provide an excellent weapon for the Free French Forces until the end of the war.

It is a well designed and well balanced arm suitable for bayonet fighting, although it is too long to be really effective as a fighting knife. It was normally carried at the side in a leather belt frog, but some French Colonial mounted troops wore it slung diagonally across their chests when equipped with the 8mm M 1892 Carbine.

The original composition grips were replaced by wood in 1914 and are held in place by larger rivets. In 1915 the swept forward quillons were shortered to the length shown. This modification was carried out to all bayonets on issue to the armed forces, although many escaped the official orders and remained unaltered.

There are several interesting features on this weapon. The blade, which is polished bright, has two notches just below the fullers which engage the scabbard blade retaining springs. The flat blade back is fullered to

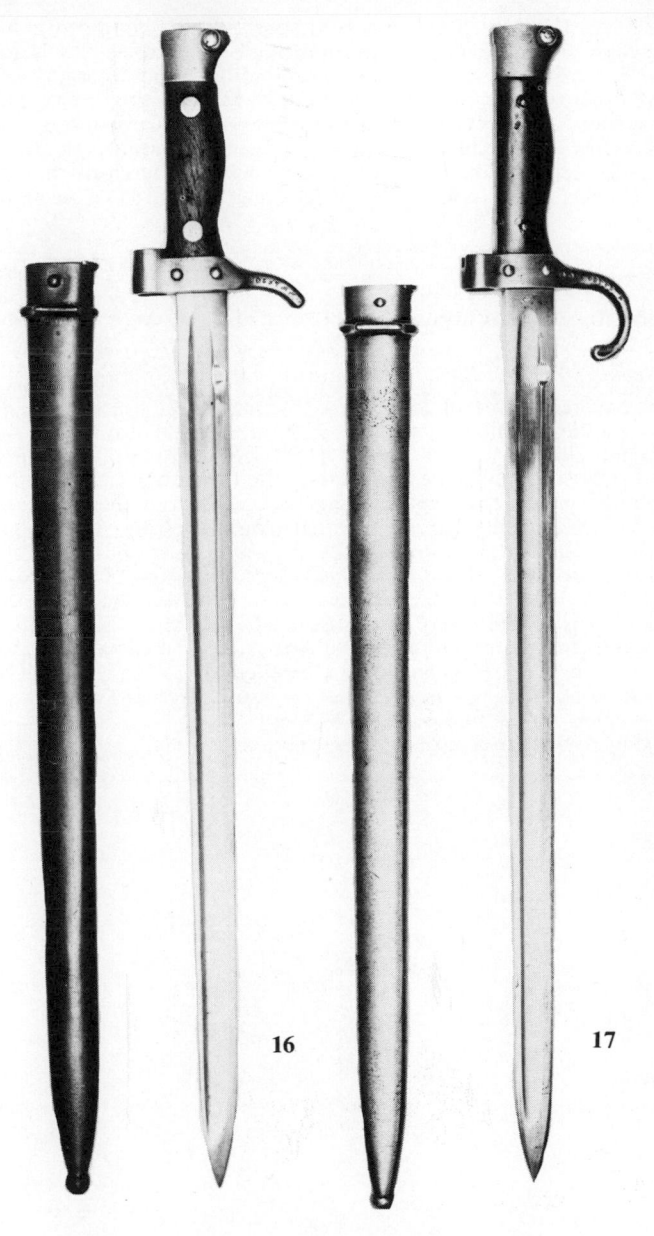

16   17

29

the point for the last 6¼in. The rifle attachment bar is engaged in a hole placed centrally in the flat pommel, and the broad muzzle ring has a cut out for half its length so that it slides around the barrel foresight.

In all other respects with its shaped hilt and fullered single edged blade, this bayonet is conventional in design, but its unusual features make it an interesting weapon in bayonet development. It is principally a carbine bayonet for artillery and mounted troops, but was superior in every way to the weapon issued to the infantry, the long Model 1886 Epée Bayonet.

Blade length: 15¾in
Overall length: 20¼in
Muzzle ring diameter: 13mm
Rifle: Model 1892 Carbine, Model 1892/27 Carbine

17. *Model 1892 Knife Bayonet* (see illustration on previous page)

This bayonet is one of the original Model 1892s which were still in use during the war though most had been modified before 1939.

This particular bayonet has the original composition grips held in place by two small rivets and the complete quillon. The muzzle ring does not overlap the grips. The broader ring was introduced to strengthen the method of attachment whereby it slotted around the foresight for a greater distance and therefore improved the steady attachment of the bayonet.

The scabbard was originally heavily blued. A very few of these bayonets were signed and dated along the back of the blade. The only example examined was marked Mre. d'Armes de Chatt. Mai 1893 which is an abbreviated form of Manufacture d'Armes de Chatellerault Mai 1893, thus showing that it was made at Chatellerault in May 1893. Though this method of marking was always carried out on earlier French bayonets it is extremely rare to find it on the Model 1892.

All dimensions are as given for the previous bayonet.

18, *Model 1936 MAS Bayonet*

In 1936 France adopted a new 7·5 cal rifle, the MAS, and equipped it with a simple rod bayonet similar to those tried and abandoned by the Americans at the beginning of the century.

The rifle and bayonet were named the MAS after the French arsenal at St. Etienne. The initials MAS stand for Manufacture d'Armes de St. Etienne.

As a bayonet it could be used effectively as a simple thrusting weapon but it could serve no other purpose as, having no hilt, it was useless as a knife. The knurled surface between the two catches was intended to facilitate holding the bayonet while placing it in position. The short cruciform blade shows that the French still considered that their blade design, originally used on the Model 1886 and earlier on socket bayonets, was still ideal for a thrusting weapon.

The bayonet is attached in fixed bayonets position by a tube under the barrel. The end catch enters this and the rod up to the knurled part when the sprung catch holds it in position. When the bayonet is not in use it is reversed and the whole blade slides down the tube. In this way the catch nearest the blade prevents it from falling out of the tube. Consequently this tube is also the scabbard so at all times the bayonet was carried on the rifle.

The same bayonet was used in a similar manner with the M 36 CR 39 Rifle which had a folding stock made of aluminium.

Blade length: 13¼in
Overall length: 17in
Rifles: 7·5mm Model 1936 MAS and Model 1936 CR 39

31

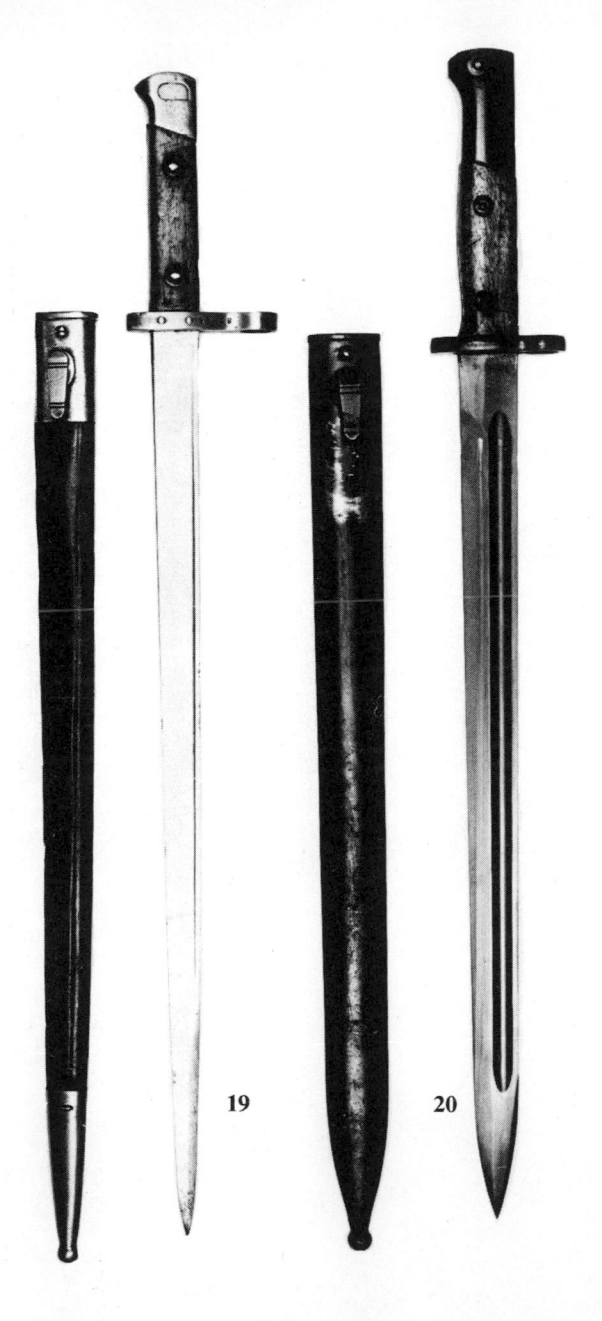

19   20

19. *Model 1903 Bayonet*

The Greek army, which inflicted crushing defeats on the invading Italians, humiliated Mussolini in his abortive attempt to present Hitler with a *fait accompli*. The small Greek army fought against overwhelming odds with great courage but were eventually defeated by German troops sent in to finish a task which had proved far too much for their Axis allies.

Greek troops were equipped in some cases with their relatively new Belgian made Model 1924 Mausers, but many still carried the Models 1903 and 1903/14 Männlicher–Schoenauers used during World War I. The bayonet used on the rifles was the Model 1903, which used a slender T backed blade similar to that of the French Gras Bayonet Model 1874. This slim tapering blade ended in a double-edged point and was best suited to thrusting. The hilt, of Austrian design, was very similar to the Austrian Model 1895 knife bayonet. During the 1914–18 War many of these bayonets made by Steyr were re-equipped with Mauser hilts and issued to the German Army.

The left blade flat is stamped with Steyr's trademark OE WG. The crossguard has a serial number 8384A and the pommel, close to the press stud, has the Greek marking of St. George killing the dragon.

The steel mounted black leather scabbard is similar in design to German scabbards and is marked by a small cross within a circle on the frog stud. All metal parts including the blade are finished bright.

Blade length: 15¼in
Overall length: 19⅝in
Muzzle ring diameter: 14mm
Weight: 13oz
Rifles: 6·5mm Männlicher–Schoenauer Models 1903 and 1903/14

20. *Model 1924 Bayonet*

The Belgian Fabrique Nationale factory supplied many nations with small arms between the wars. All the bayonets followed a similar pattern differing only in blade length and muzzle ring diameter. In 1924 Greece bought from Belgium numbers of Mauser rifles and bayonets to replace some of their Männlicher–Schoenauer Models 1903 and 1903/14 rifles.

The bayonet issued to the Greek army with this rifle is typically Belgian. It has a conventional long single edged blade which is double edged at the point. This is parkerised to a dark dull finish while the hilt is heavily blued. The pommel has a Mauser pattern bar attachment groove, but unlike German Mauser bayonets is also equipped with a muzzle ring. The whole bayonet is conventional in design but is unusual only in that it has a longer blade than those short knife bayonets favoured by other countries during this period.

The scabbard which is also heavily blued overall is German in design even to the frog stud, although made by F.N.

The only marking is the number B 5246 stamped on the pommel by the Belgian factory.

Blade length: 15⅛in
Overall length: 20¼in
Muzzle ring diameter: 15·5mm
Weight: 16oz
Rifle: Greek Model 1924 FN Mauser

21. Greek troops in action, against Italians in 1942, with Model 1903 bayonet.

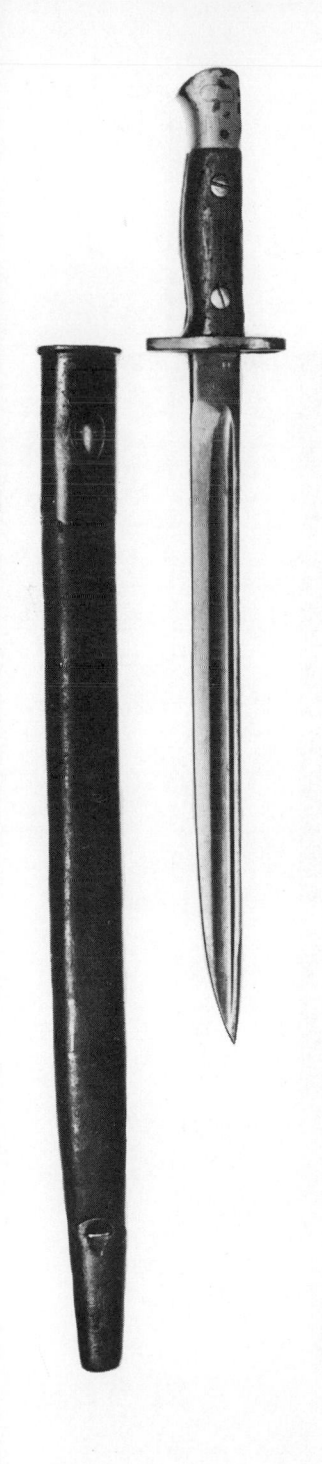

22. *Pattern Mk 1**

This bayonet which is a shortened and altered U.K. Pattern 1907 was India's first attempt to produce a weapon more suitable for jungle warfare against the Japanese than the original model. Few of these were manufactured but they served as prototypes for the widely produced Indian Pattern bayonets.

By shortening the original 17in blade to one of exactly 12in a new weapon with all the advantages of a knife bayonet was easily and cheaply made. It was better balanced for use as a knife and more easily wielded in the confines of close combat in thick vegetation.

The last five inches of blade were cut off and the point reshaped to the original design of the P 07. Some were made with the false edge shown on this model and others without it. Blades thus altered are readily distinguished from later models by the presence of the P 07 fullers, which continue to the point. The blades were then heavily reblued. The hilts were left unaltered but were usually painted khaki on all metal parts including the grip retaining screws.

Most of the original markings on the blade have been removed by refinishing but on the left side they are just visible. There is the pattern mark 1907 over the date of manufacture, 1 '14 for January 1914. Below this the manufacturer's mark EFD for Enfield. On the right side are the new marks more crudely stamped in larger figures, Mk I* and 11 41, showing that it was converted in November 1941. All others examined were produced within a few months of this date. They were carried in their original unaltered scabbards.

Blade length: 12in
Overall length: 16¾in
Muzzle ring diameter: 17mm
Weight: 13oz
Rifle: S.M.L.E.

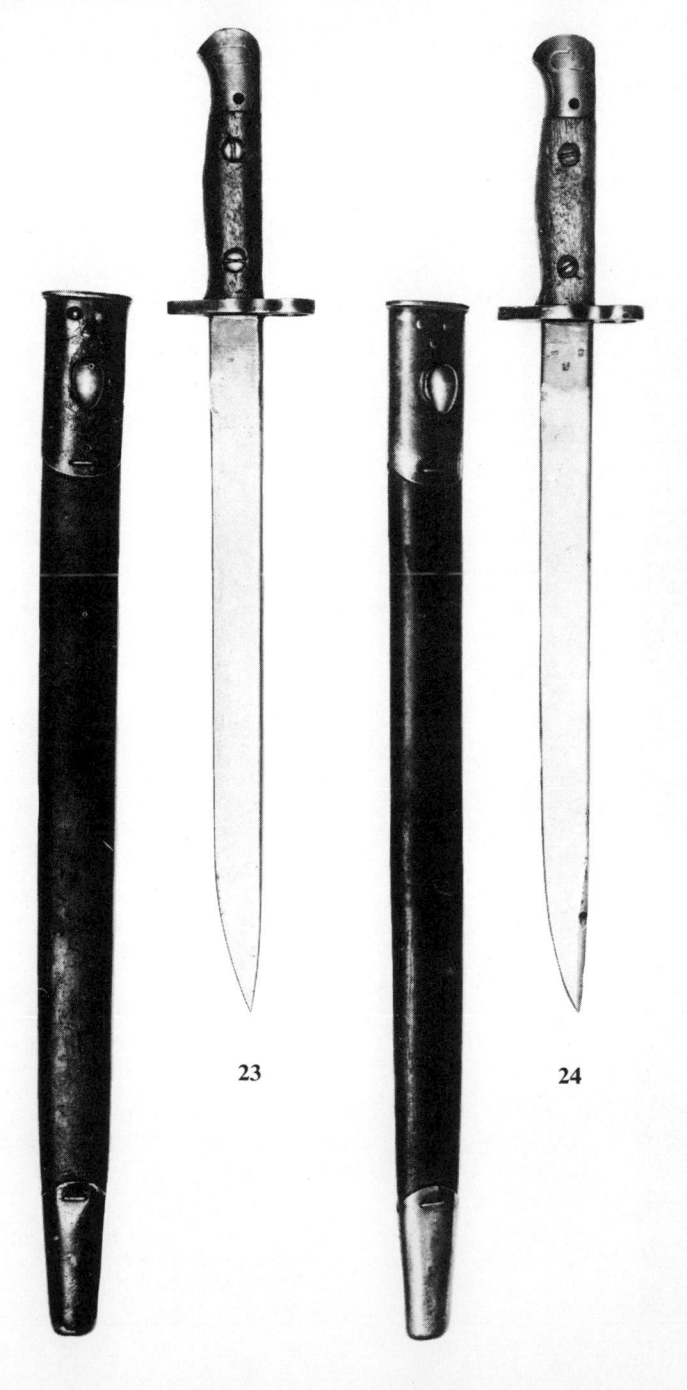

23   24

23 and **24.** *Pattern Bayonets Mk I and Mk II*

From 1941 to the end of the war Indian arms factories produced bayonets made up from parts sent out from Britain. The 12in blades were produced in India and although each weapon is stamped on the blade as being a particular Mark, these designations were never strictly adhered to, with the result that two identical bayonets may be stamped as different Marks.

The first of these bayonets were produced in 1941 and were made with a false edge to the blade. Some of these may be found stamped Mk I* and others marked in this way are overstamped Mk II. It appears that the original shortened Pattern 1907s were designated Mk I* and that in some cases the first of the new models erroneously carried this stamp. The great majority of these false-edged bayonets are dated 1942 or 1943 and are stamped Mk II.

The example illustrated which always has the new blade without fullers is stamped on the left blade flat with G.R.I. below the crown, under this Mk II, the date 5 42 for May 1942 and the Ishapore factory mark R.F.I. The right blade flat has the India Stores marks.

The second example made without the false edge to the blade is stamped on the left blade flat in crude lettering Mk II above the date 7 43 for July 1943 and the manufacturer's mark J U.

The majority of those without the false edge were manufactured at a later date than those with the false edge. The Ishapore factory were producing both types in early 1942.

The hilts of these bayonets, which are original parts for the Pattern 1907 bayonet, are heavily blued while in most cases the blades are finished bright. The scabbards are again those originally made for the Pattern 1907 (No I Mk I) and were not shortened until after the war.

Blade length: 12in
Overall length: 16⅝in
Muzzle ring diameter: 17mm
Weight: 13oz.
Rifle: S.M.L.E.

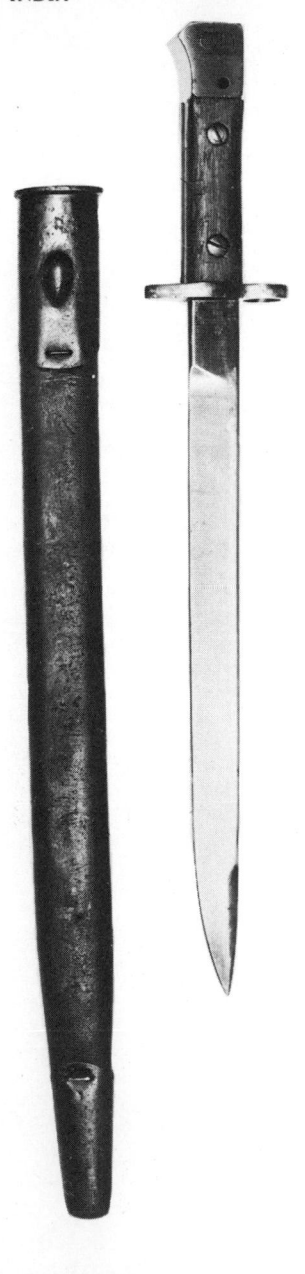

25. *Pattern Bayonets Mk II and Mk III (Unfinished Models)*

The example illustrated is one of the bayonets manufactured towards the end of the war in 1944 and 1945, although a very few are dated 1943. As speed of production was most important these bayonets were issued before they reached the final stages of manufacture. The hilt has not been shaped to fit the hand and the pommel edges have been left square and sharp.

This bayonet is heavily blued and the blade has a short false edge at the point. It is stamped on the left blade flat with G.R.I. under a crown, below this Mk II, the date 8 44 for August 1944 and the Ishapore factory mark R.F.I. The right blade flat has the India Stores marks. Other identical models are stamped Mk III and these are usually dated 1945.

Those examples examined without the false edge have been stamped Mk II and dated 1943 and 1944.

These were all issued with the full length unshortened scabbards.

    Blade length: 12in
    Overall length: 16⅜in
    Muzzle ring diameter: 17mm
    Weight: 13oz
    Rifle: S.M.L.E.

26. *Model 1895 Rifle Bayonet*

This is the standard infantry bayonet issued with the Männlicher infantry rifle which was the equipment of the majority of Dutch troops who fought the German armies in 1940. The Dutch forces fought against overwhelming odds and surrendered on May 14th after four days of bitter fighting, although some units held out until the 17th. Any attempt to continue to withstand the invasion, which was sweeping aside the allied Dutch, Belgian and French armies in the low countries would have led merely to the senseless slaughter of the remaining Dutch forces.

The bayonets and rifles were still those first adopted in 1895, but they were far from obsolete in 1940. This infantry bayonet has a strong single-edged T-backed blade with a double-edged point. This tapering blade was ideal for thrusting although all edges were left relatively blunt and were consequently of little real use for cutting.

The hilt is very similar to that of the British Pattern 1888 bayonets in that the T shaped bar attachment groove is positioned in the lower side of the pommel and the back of the pommel is curved to fit close to the barrel. This method of attachment combined with the muzzle ring ensures a very sturdy form of attachment. The plain wood grips are held in place by two large steel rivets.

The leather scabbard has a permanently attached belt frog held in place by copper rivets with brass washers. It is also equipped with a loop to hold the bayonet in the scabbard. A brass ferrule reinforces the leather point.

This particular bayonet is stamped on the left blade flat HEMBRUG where it was manufactured in Holland. The right flat and pommel are marked with a small crowned e and there is a serial number 7135 R on the crossguard. All metal parts are finished in a dark blue.

Blade length: 14½in
Overall length: 18⅞in
Muzzle ring diameter: 14·5mm
Weight: 12oz
Rifle: 6·5mm Model 1895
   Männlicher Infantry Rifle

27. Model 1895 Rifle Bayonet with stacking hook

This bayonet is the earliest model of the previous bayonet described since the swept forward quillon was abandoned gradually after the 1914–18 War. Those bayonets without quillons were made between the wars and some of the original pattern had their quillons removed.

The Dutch did not design the "quillon" to catch an opponent's blade in combat. The purpose was to facilitate stacking the rifles by interlocking the "quillons." However this pronounced hook was found in practice to be more of a hindrance than a useful refinement. The Dutch were also influenced by the international trend to abandon the quillon for, during World War I both Britain and France had modified their bayonets in this manner.

This particular bayonet was made before World War I in Austria. There is no visible difference in manufacture except for the factory's mark of OE WG on the left blade flat, which is Steyr's abbreviated trademark for Oesterreichische Waffenfabrik Ges. The right flat and pommel are stamped with a small crowned T and there is the serial number on the crossguard, 6792 N.

All dimensions are as given for the previous model.

28. Model 1895 Carbine Bayonet— Cavalry

The mounted troops of the Dutch army were first issued with bayonets in 1895, and these differed completely in design from other models of the time. Instead of the T-backed blade this knife bayonet featured a slim double-edged blade ideal for thrusting or cutting in either direction. It is diamond shaped in cross section and closely resembles the blades of South European stilettos.

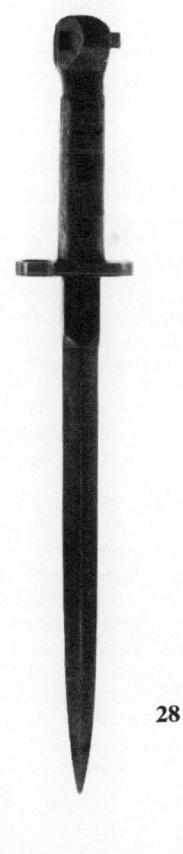

The hilt grips are slim and straight, but the bulbous pommel and crossguard enable the bayonet to be gripped comfortably and firmly when used as a fighting knife.

The scabbard issued with this bayonet is similar in design to all Dutch scabbards. Made completely of leather it has an integral belt frog with catch and a steel ferrule sewn inside the leather body.

The left blade flat is stamped HEMBRUG where it was manufactured. The left flat has a small crowned Z which also appears on the pommel. The serial number 5397 H is stamped on the crossguard.

Blade length: 9⅞in
Overall length: 14⅝in
Muzzle ring diameter: 14·5mm
Rifle: 6·5mm Model 1895
    Männlicher Carbine No 1

Model 1895 Carbine Bayonet— Cavalry (Variations)

Like the infantry bayonet the Cavalry model was originally issued with a stacking hook on the crossguard. These were gradually removed after the 1914–18 War and those made thereafter were as described above without the hook.

Between the wars just a few were manufactured with composition grips, and these replaced the original plain wood models.

Some of the Dutch Cavalry were armed with a socket bayonet. This is a shortened version of the bayonet originally issued with the 11mm Model 1871 Beaumont Rifle. It is a conventional model with locking ring and cruciform blade with an overall length of 17·25in (43·7cm). It was issued with the Model 1895 Carbine No 1 old model.

28

41

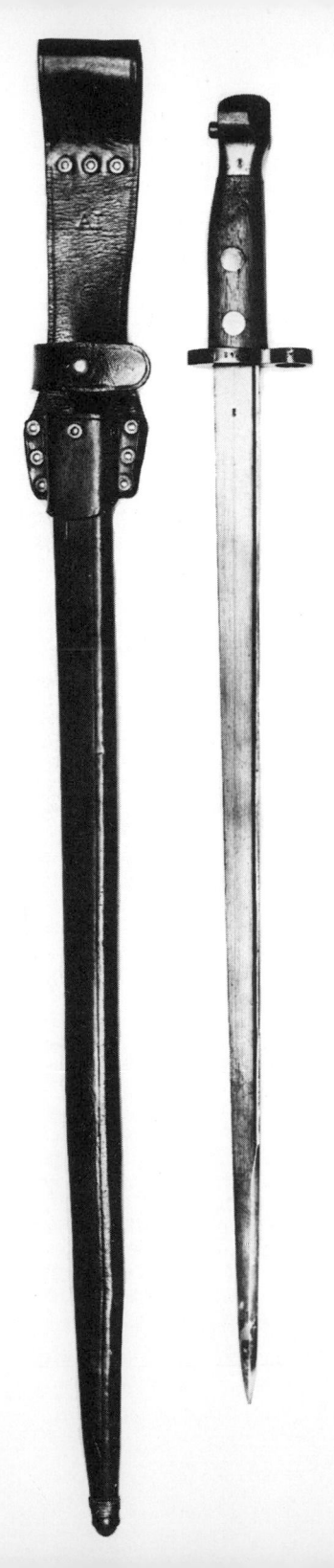

Model 1895 Carbine Folding Bayonet

The Dutch Military Police were issued with the Model 1895 Carbine No 2, which was equipped with a folding bayonet which had a cruciform blade 12in long and an overall length of 14·09in. This weapon was issued in very limited quantities.

29. *Model 1895 Carbine Bayonet*

This large illustration is reproduced in scale with the Netherlands bayonets on pp. 39 and 40.

This bayonet which is similar in all respects to the preceding models except for its blade length was issued to the Dutch engineers, artillery troops and cyclists. Its additional reach compensated for the comparatively short carbine carried by these troops while its weight and shape did not detract from its excellent qualities as an easily wielded thrusting weapon.

The hilt is identical to that of the previous model described and was only manufactured with a straight crossguard without a quillon. The long slim blade with its strong T back has a double edged point. However, although it has a single edge it is only suited for thrusting, since the edge and the point are blunt. All metal surfaces are heavily dark blued.

The left flat of the blade is stamped HEMBRUG where the bayonet was made. The right flat and pommel are stamped with a small crowned Z and there is a serial number 7742 L on the crossguard.

The unstained brown leather scabbard has its frog stud permanently attached by 11 copper rivets and brass washers. The belt loop is also formed with three rivets and two more hold the leather catch in position. The scabbard tip has a brass ferrule sewn inside so that only the round point protrudes. Copper wire wound round the leather reinforces the point.

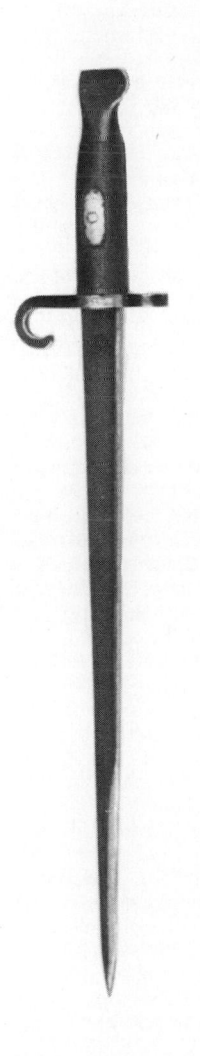

The scabbard is marked with a crowned S in a circle and the mark A I on the loop.

Blade length: 19in
Overall length: 23¾in
Muzzle ring diameter: 14·5mm
Weight: 12oz
Rifle: 6·5mm Model 1895
Mannlicher Carbines
Nos 3 and 4

30. *Model 1895 Rifle Bayonet for Marines*

The bayonet issued to Dutch Marines was identical to the infantry bayonet with stacking hook except for one difference. The plain wood grips were held in place by a single bolt and an oblong steel washer on either side. These large washers are 3cm long. It was manufactured by the Steyr factory and bears their trademark on the left blade flat. There is a small crowned T on the right flat and on the pommel.

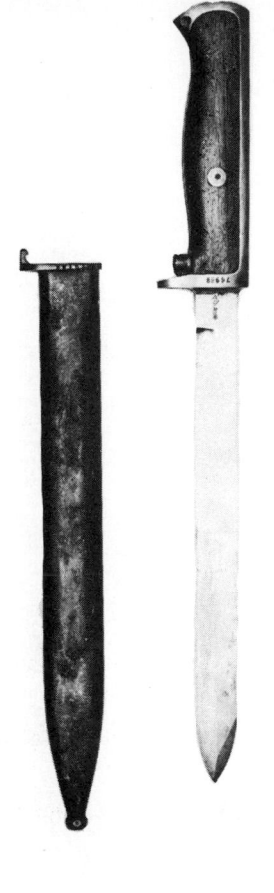

31. *Model 1894 Knife Bayonet*

This knife bayonet and the long knife bayonets, although first issued in 1894 with the 6·5mm Krag-Jorgensen Rifle were still the standard infantry bayonets of the Norwegian armed forces during the war. As Norway had pursued a policy of peaceful neutrality and was unaffected by any aggressive policies the expenditure on armaments had been kept to a minimum. Thus when Norway was attacked by Germany on 9th April 1940, the bayonets in use with the Norwegian forces were the Model 1894s. During the short campaign which ended on June 10th these arms were used with great courage against the overwhelming German forces and were used alongside British and French troops at the battle of Narvik.

All this family of bayonets have an interesting manufacturing process in that the blade and hilt are formed from one piece of steel. Consequently there is no blade tang as there is no need to hold the blade in position. It was easy to produce since there are only six separate steel parts to manufacture. The bolt that holds the two plain wood grips in position also acts as a pivot for the catch which is placed internally. The press stud acts as a retaining catch holding the bayonet securely in the scabbard as well as operating the bar catch which pivots into the bar attachment groove. This method was found to be so steady that no muzzle ring was provided. The back of the hilt is curved so that it fits close to the barrel.

The single edged knife blade has no fullers and ends in a spear point with the last inch of the blade back sharpened to improve the point for thrusting.

The short steel scabbard is heavily blued. A leather belt frog attached as on the other models illustrated clips over the stud on the scabbard near the mouthpiece.

Blade length: 8⅜in
Overall length: 13⅛in
Rifles: 6·5mm M 1894
    Krag-Jorgensen,
    M 1912 Carbine,
    M 1925 Sharpshooter's Rifle

32. *Model 1894—Leather Scabbard*

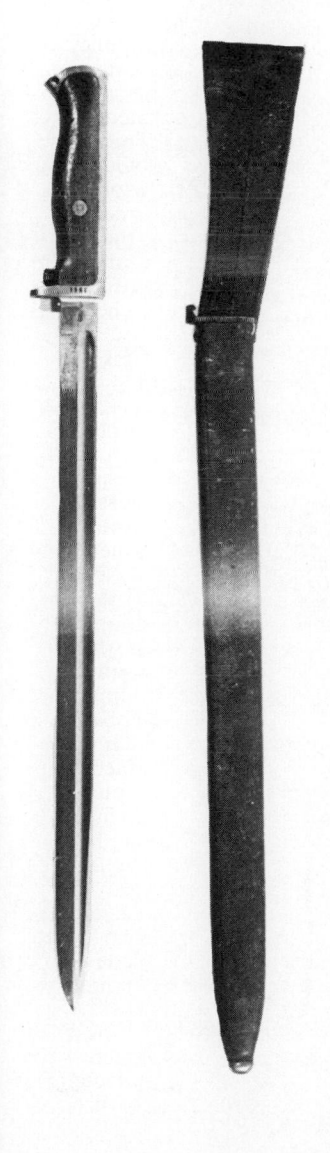

This is the long knife bayonet used by the Norwegian forces up to their surrender in 1940.

It has the same hilt and single-edged blade used on all the Model 1894 series of bayonets but this particular weapon has long fullers which run to the point of the blade. The fullers gradually taper towards the point for the last quarter of the blade length.

This bayonet was made at Konsberg and has a crowned K stamped on the blade. A serial number appears on the crossguard. After 1905–06 a crowned H7 also appears on the bayonet. Other bayonets were manufactured on contract by Steyr in Austria and by Husqvarna in Sweden who made 2000 bayonets in 1894 and 1895. The great majority of rifles and bayonets were made at Konsberg while Steyr produced 29,000.

It is equipped with the leather scabbard with integral belt frog. The mouthpiece with catch and the ferrule are steel.

When under the German occupation these bayonets were shortened the leather scabbards were also cut down.

Blade length: 14½in
Overall length: 19¼in
Rifles: 6·5mm M 1894
    Krag-Jorgensen,
    M 1912 Carbine,
    M 1925 Sharpshooter's Rifle

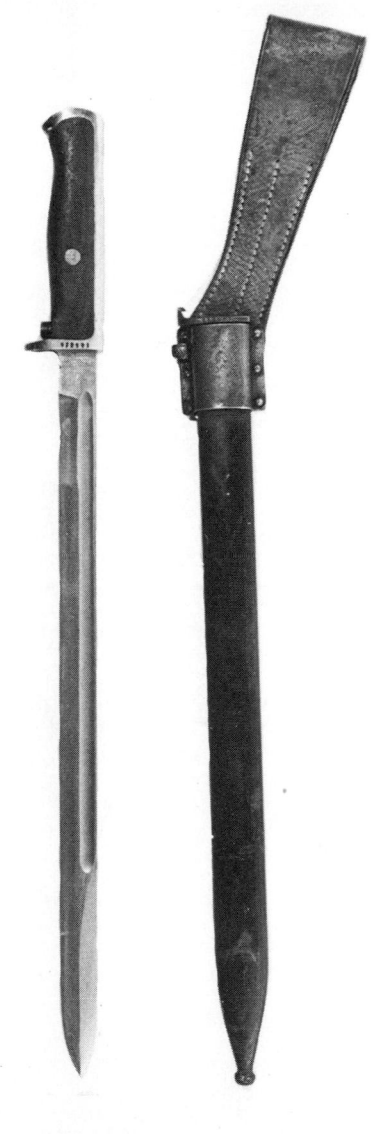

33. *Model 1894—Steel Scabbard*

This bayonet is a variation of the previous model described and differs only in its blade form. On this model the fullers are shorter and end well before the point which is sharpened to a double edge. This gives the bayonet a more conventional blade design and is an improvement over the long model with fullers that run out at the point. Not only is it stronger but it combines a long cutting edge with the ability to cut on an upwards sweep. Together these factors provide an excellent double edged point ideal for thrusting.

This model is equipped with the long steel scabbard which features a leather belt frog with a diagonal loop held in place by a steel plate and catch.

Some of these bayonets were shortened during the German occupation.

Blade length: 14½in
Overall length: 19¼in
Rifles: 6·5mm M 1894
    Krag-Jorgensen,
    M 1912 Carbine,
    M 1925 Sharpshooter's Rifle

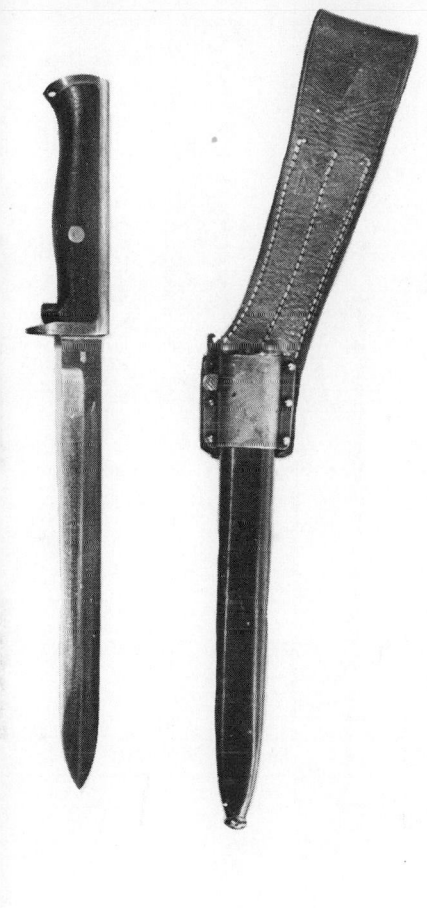

34. *Model 1894 Knife Bayonet—
modified*

This bayonet illustrated is a shortened modification of the long Model
1894. The original model had its
fullers running the full length of the
blade. However during the German
occupation of Norway from 1940–45
the German authorities ordered that
the Norwegians should shorten their
bayonets to bring them in line with
the short knife weapons favoured by
the Germans. The modification was
carried out simply by cutting part of
the blade away and regrinding the
remaining part to the original point
shape. This regrinding was usually
done without attention to detail so
that the machine marks are clearly
visible on the point.

The scabbard shown is a short
blackened steel model with a leather
belt frog which has a diagonal loop.
When hanging from the belt this
points the hilt forward and up so
that it is carried in exactly the
perfect position for withdrawing the
bayonet. The press stud on this
model is removed by gripping it and
twisting to unscrew it, whereas the
previous model had the stud cut
across the top to facilitate removal
by screwdriver.

Blade length: 8½in
Overall length: 13¼in
Weight: 8oz

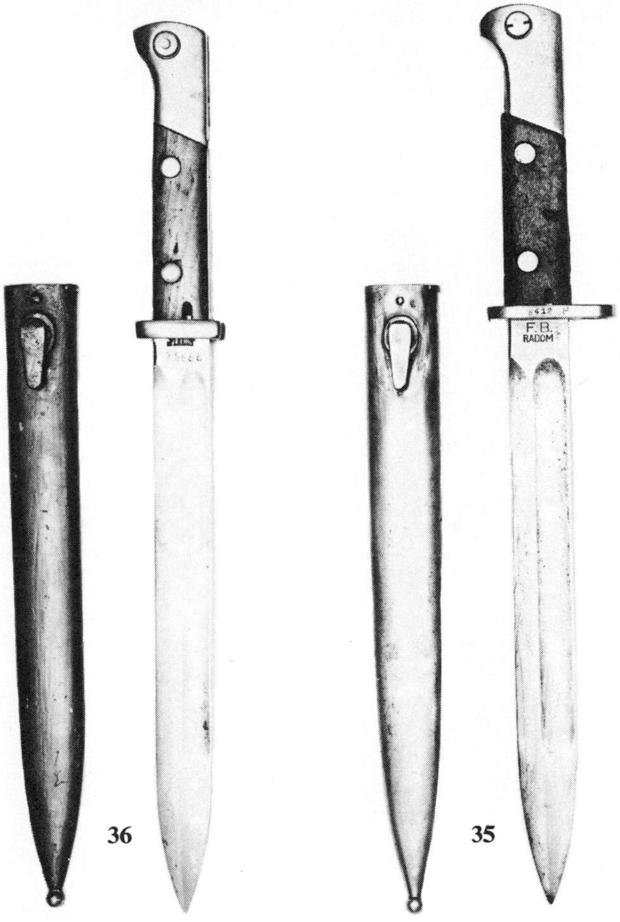

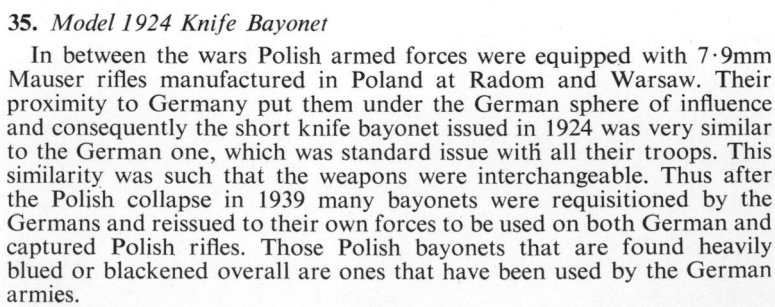

36   35

35. *Model 1924 Knife Bayonet*

In between the wars Polish armed forces were equipped with 7·9mm Mauser rifles manufactured in Poland at Radom and Warsaw. Their proximity to Germany put them under the German sphere of influence and consequently the short knife bayonet issued in 1924 was very similar to the German one, which was standard issue with all their troops. This similarity was such that the weapons were interchangeable. Thus after the Polish collapse in 1939 many bayonets were requisitioned by the Germans and reissued to their own forces to be used on both German and captured Polish rifles. Those Polish bayonets that are found heavily blued or blackened overall are ones that have been used by the German armies.

The main difference in design which is immediately obvious if a Polish and German bayonet are compared is that the wood grips on the Polish model meet the steel pommel diagonally rather than vertically.

This bayonet illustrated is one made with a muzzle ring which is a feature not found on German bayonets. However this does not affect their interchangeability. The plain beechwood grips slightly overlap the blade tang as on this particular model no steel flashguard has been fitted along the back of the grips. The blade and hilt are in their original condition and are polished bright. The steel scabbard was originally painted khaki.

Some of these bayonets are stamped on the pommel WZ 24 (WZ is the Polish abbreviation for Model). This particular bayonet is stamped with a serial number on the crossguard 5412 P. The right flat of the blade is marked F.B. above RADOM and the left flat has the Polish eagle above the letters W.P.

Blade length: 10in
Overall length: 15·2in
Muzzle ring diameter: 15·5mm
Weight: 16oz
Rifle: Mauser
Variation: Made also with a flashguard

36. *Model 1924 Knife Bayonet (2)*

This model, although a distinct variation from the previous bayonet described, fits the same rifle and can be used equally well on German Mauser rifles.

It differs in that it has no muzzle ring and is also equipped with a flashguard along the back of the grips. The top of the crossguard is left curved so that when it is attached to the rifle it keeps the bayonet steady by resting firmly against the barrel. The plain grips are well fitting and do not overlap the tang. A slight variation can be seen in the press stud which is not cut to allow removal by a special screwdriver.

This bayonet is in its original condition with polished steel parts and a painted khaki scabbard.

Manufacturing tolerances were never strictly adhered to and consequently slight variations are common especially in the width of the tang and grips of the hilt. Furthermore this type of bayonet was also manufactured without a flashguard.

This particular model has the serial number 75688 on the right blade flat below the manufacturer's name PERKUN. Next to this is an S in a square. The left blade flat has the Polish eagle above the letters W.P.

Blade length: 10in
Overall length: 15¼in
Weight: 16oz
Rifle: Mauser
Variation: Made also without a flashguard

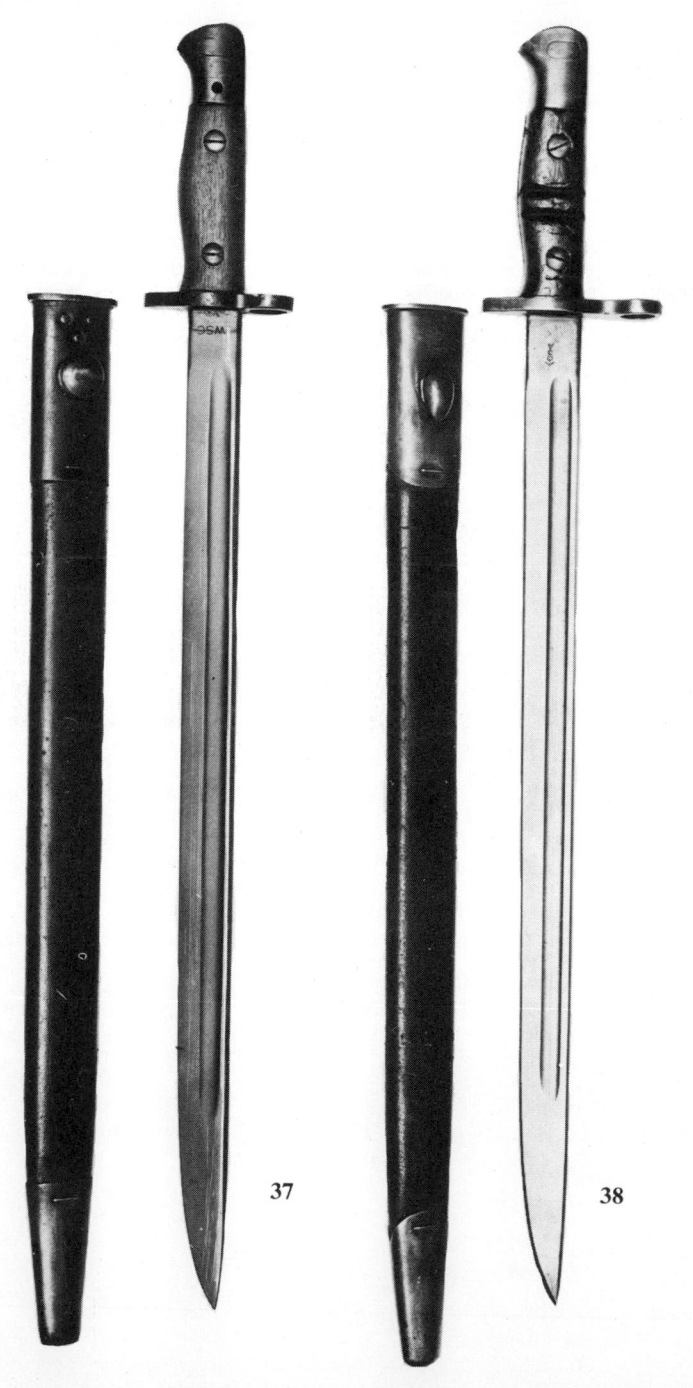

37

38

37. *No 1 Mk 1 Bayonet (Pattern 1907)*

During World War II many S.M.L.E. rifles remained in service, although they had been superseded by the No 4 Mk 1 rifle equipped with the No 4 spike bayonets. These S.M.L.E. rifles, which saw action in all theatres of war from Europe and Africa to the Pacific, were equipped with the most famous of British bayonets the Pattern 1907, redesignated No 1 Mk 1 in 1926. This bayonet was the standard infantry bayonet of all British forces during the 1914–18 war. Originally made with a swept forward quillon and no oil cleaning hole it was modified in 1913 by the removal of the quillon. After this new models were manufactured with oil holes in the pommels, and these bayonets were the final type and were used during the 1939–45 war.

Millions of these bayonets were produced—the majority by the firms of Vickers, Mole, Wilkinson Sword, Chapman, Sanderson, Remington (U.S.A.) and the Enfield Arsenal. Others were made in India and Australia. Most were made with bright polished blades, but others were parkerised or heavily blued to prevent reflection. Hilts were similarly finished, although many were painted khaki.

This particular bayonet, which has a parkerised blade and blued hilt, has the manufacturer's name WILKINSON on the left blade flat below the date of manufacture 12 18 for December 1918. Above this is the pattern mark 1907 below a crowned G.R. for Georgius Rex. The date '36 appears with inspection marks showing that it was reproofed in 1936. The right blade flat has the examiner's marks on either side of the X below the final acceptance mark of the War Department broad arrow. The pommel is stamped R.E. 206 CO. 62 for 206th Company, Royal Engineers, Weapon No 62.

The scabbards were all leather and the steel mounts were painted black or khaki or heavily blued.

Blade length: 17in; Overall length: 21¾in; Muzzle ring diameter: 17mm; Weight: 18oz; Rifle: S.M.L.E

38. *No 3 Mk 1 Bayonet (Pattern 1913)*

The Pattern 1913 bayonet which was manufactured for Britain by the American firms of Eddystone, Winchester and Remington was reissued during the 1939–45 war with the Pattern 1914 rifle. Many more were converted and used to make pikes for the Home Guard.

This bayonet is very similar to the American Pattern 1917 bayonet; the only difference apart from markings is that officially the British bayonet has no oil cleaning hole in the pommel while the American model has this feature. (Control was not as strict as it should have been, with the result that some bayonets sent to Britain as P 13s did have cleaning holes.) Some American P 17 bayonets have British markings and these are some that were sent to Britain during World War II as part of the U.S. lend-lease programme. (Some P 13s intended for Britain were requisitioned by the Americans for their P 17 rifles during the first war and consequently have cancelled British marks with American markings added.)

Basically the Pattern 1913 is very similar to the Pattern 1907. The blade is the same, but the hilt crossguard has the muzzle ring further from the hilt. The wood grips differ in that there are two deep grooves cut across their width to avoid any confusion with the Pattern 1907. The steel mounted leather scabbards are the same as those for the P 07 bayonet.

This particular bayonet is stamped on the left flat of the blade with the manufacturers mark REMINGTON within a circle. Above this is the date of manufacture 5 17 for May 1917 below the Pattern mark 1913. On the right blade flat there are two examiner's stamps on either side of an X and above these the broad arrow War Department acceptance mark. The blade is parkerised but the hilt and crossguard are lightly blued.

Blade length: 17in; Overall length: 21¾in; Muzzle ring diameter: 15·5mm; Weight: 1lb 2oz; Rifle: British Pattern 1914 Rifle; Interchangeable with U.S. Pattern 1917 ·30–06 rifle

No 4 Mk I
(see plate 40)

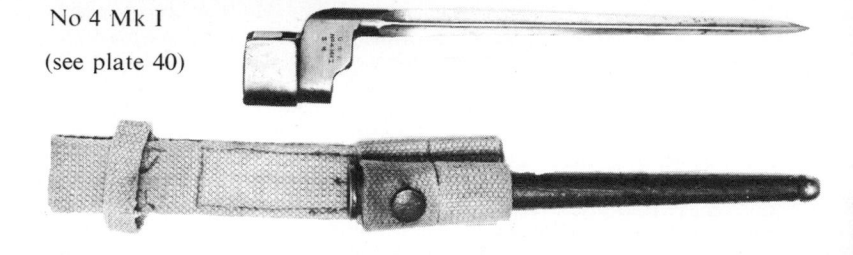

No 4 Mk II
(see plate 41)

No 4 Mk II*
(see plate 43)

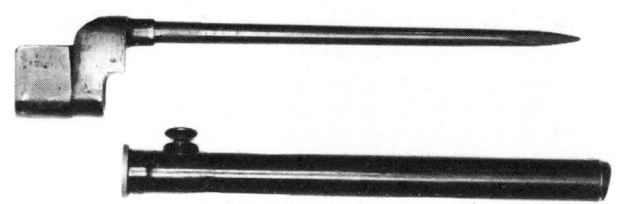

No 4 Mk III
(see plate 44)

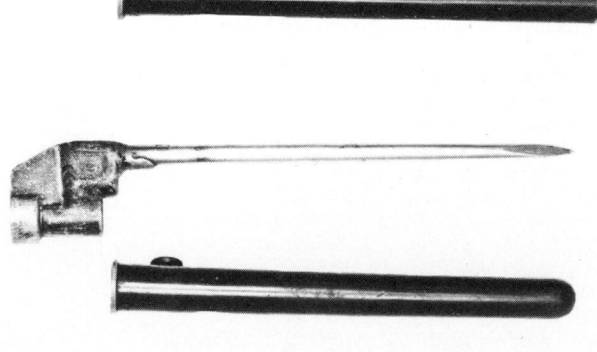

39. *Bayonets and scabbards*—comparative lengths

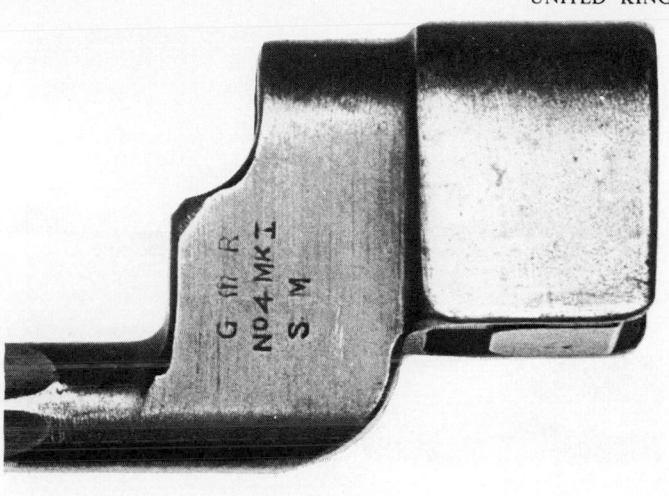

40. *No 4 Mk I Bayonet*

This short spike bayonet with its cruciform blade was first officially approved in November 1939, although tests of the spike bayonets had started as early as 1925. Though no hilt was provided which precluded any use of the weapon as a knife or sword, it did fulfil its purpose solely as a bayonet.

The cruciform blade which tapers to a point, is finished bright and the socket is heavily blued. This socket slides over the barrel muzzle and is held in place by a barrel lug, which is engaged by a sliding sprung press stud in the socket body.

The socket is stamped G R with a crown between the two letters below this No 4 Mk I and the letters S M.

The scabbard shown here is the Mk I adopted at the same time as the bayonet and issued with the majority of all No 4 bayonets throughout the war. It is painted khaki and has no markings. It has a removable mouthpiece, which holds the blade retaining springs. At the end of the round tapering steel body is a round ferrule which has a drain hole.

Blade length: 7⅞in
Overall length: 9⅞in
Weight: 7oz
Rifle: ·303 No 4 Mk I* and Sten Submachine Gun

41. *No 4 Mk II Bayonet*

This model differs from the preceding Mk I in that the blade is no longer cruciform but is round. It tapers gradually to a point, which is machined flat on either side similar to the point of a screw-driver. As an extremely sharp and narrow point would be brittle and difficult to withdraw after penetrating bone the point has been ground off to leave a chisel-like end. These bayonets were manufactured from a one piece forging and were both cheaper and simpler to mass produce than the Mk I, which was discontinued at the outbreak of hostilities until after the war.

5 This particular bayonet was one of many made by various factories in the United States on contract to the British Government. It is stamped on the socket NO.4.MK II above an **5** which is the mark of the Stevens–Savage firm. This mark also appears on the press stud. The dull metal socket and blade are blued.

The scabbard shown was also manufactured in the U.S.A. in relatively small numbers by the firm of Victory Plastics and their trademark, ⴘ , appears on the flat back. The body is formed from black plastic, having a flat back and rounded front. It has a black steel mouth piece with a webbing frog attached by two steel press studs at the back.

Blade length: $7\frac{7}{8}$in (from point to socket)
Overall: $9\frac{7}{8}$in
Weight: 7oz
Rifle: ·303 No 4 Mk I* and Sten

42. British troops of the 14th Army in action in Burma, March 1945, with No 4 Mk I* rifle and No 4 Mk II spike bayonets.

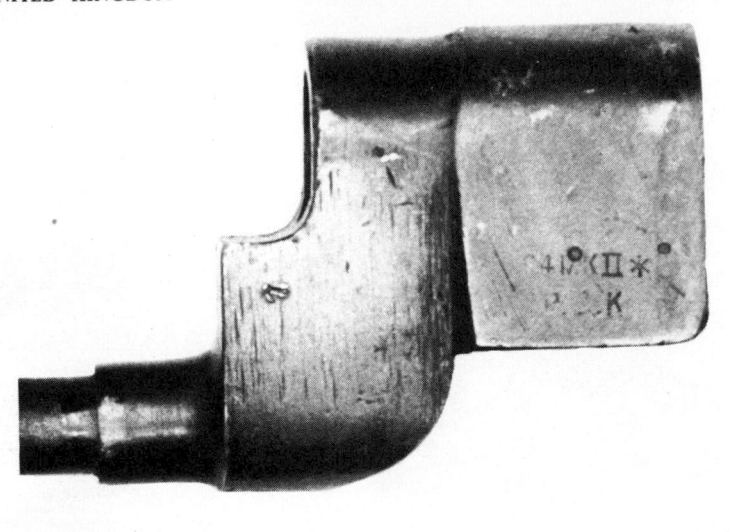

43. *No 4 Mk II* Bayonet*

This bayonet represents a development of the spike bayonet only in the manufacturing processes. It is in every way the same bayonet as the Mk II except that to facilitate forging the blade and socket were produced separately and then brazed together. This process is evident from the lip ½in below the socket.

The overall finish is better than the American made Mk II, but machine marks are visible on the socket which is blued heavily. The blade is parkerised to give a dull mat finish.

The socket of this particular specimen is stamped No 4 Mk II* above P.S.K. the trademark of Prince–Smith of Keighley in Yorkshire. This firm also manufactured many of the Mk IIs.

The scabbard shown here is the straight steel Mk II model approved in July 1943. The mouthpiece is aluminium. The steel body is painted black and marked with the War Department broad arrow. The majority of all these and the other Marks were issued with the Mk I scabbard.

Blade length: 7⅞in
Overall: 9⅞in
Weight: 7oz
Rifle: ·303 No 4 Mk I* and Sten

44. *No 4 Mk III Bayonet*

The Mk III approved in February 1943 was the last development of the No 4 bayonets though the postwar No 9 Mk I utilised the same socket with a bowie knife blade. Again the difference is basically that of the method of manufacture taking into account the wartime need to produce the same bayonet more cheaply and more quickly than the previous examples described. While this model was being introduced production of the Mk IIs continued in factories which had the Mk II tooling facilities set up.

The socket of this bayonet is made from rough dull metal in two parts. The socket was made to fine tolerances (to fit over the barrel) and was then wrapped around with sheet metal and welded together to form the hilt. The blade, again made separately, was brazed into a hole in the socket body and reinforced by a steel lip visible along the blade. The press stud was made from thin sheet metal, pressed into shape, then heavily blued. The rest of the hilt was painted black or khaki and the blade was left with a dull metal finish.

The scabbard shown in the illustration is the Mk III made of black plastic with an aluminium mouthpiece and oval plastic frog stud. There are no marks evident on this scabbard.

Blade length: $7\frac{1}{4}$in (from point to socket lip)
Overall length: $9\frac{7}{8}$in
Weight: 7oz
Rifle: ·303 No 4 Mk I* and Sten

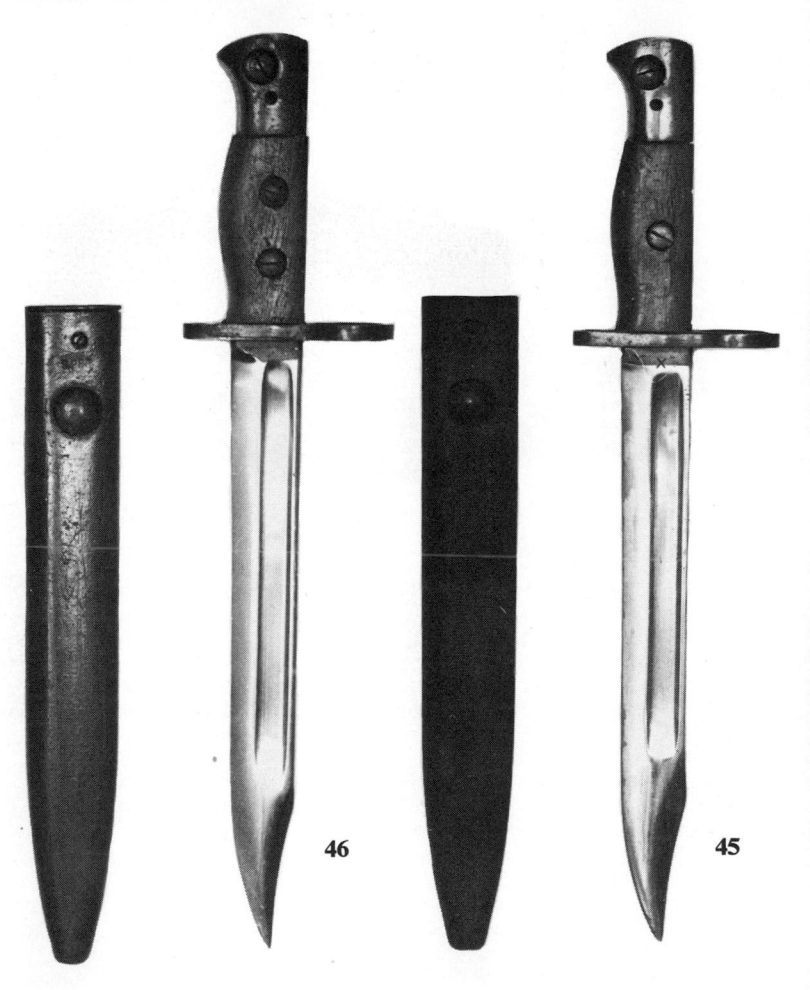

46

45

45 and **46.** *No 5 Mk I and II Jungle Carbine Bayonets*

These models provided a short knife bayonet, featuring a bowie blade, which was ideal for combat conditions in jungle warfare. The Mk I which was introduced in September 1944 differs from the Mk II which followed in early 1945 in that the grips were held in place by one screw bolt. The metal parts of the Mk I hilt are blued, whereas the Mk II is painted black. The Mk I scabbard is finished with a black crackle surface, but this was abandoned in favour of plain black paint used on the Mk II and all future models.

This type of bayonet has several interesting features. The hilt has a round groove for rifle bar attachment. The plain wood grips completely surround the blade tang. The crossguard has a large muzzle ring to fit over the flash hider on the carbine. A hole in the lower part of the guard could be used to take the end of a hand guard, which then slotted into the pommel groove when the bayonet was used as a close combat fighting knife. All parts including the scabbard were painted black except for the blade, which was finished bright.

Both examples have the letters W.S.C. for Wilkinson Sword Company on the left side of the blade and the War Department broad arrow on the right side.

Blade length: 8in
Overall length: 11⅞in
Muzzle ring diameter: 23mm
Weight: 10½oz
Rifle: ·303 No 5 Jungle Carbine Mk I and Mk I*

(Mk I, Collection: Kevin Bestt)

47. American marines in the Solomon Islands, 1942. Troops with 1903 Springfield rifles and Model 1905 bayonets.

48. *Model 1905 Bayonet*

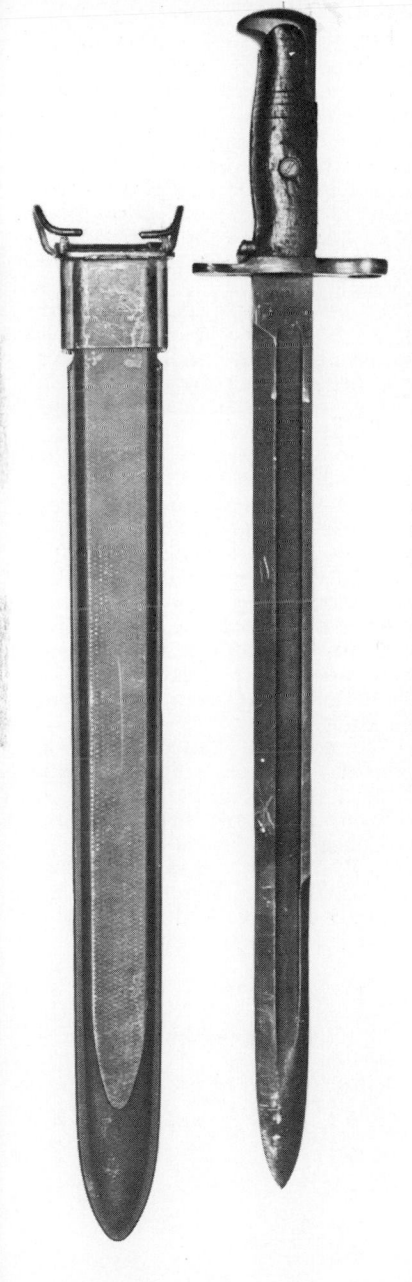

The Model 1905 bayonet first issued with the 1903 Springfield rifle was adopted after considering reports of the Russo-Japanese War and from their own experiences in the Philippines. It replaced the rod bayonet first issued with the Springfield and though modified in 1942 it remained the American soldier's infantry arm throughout two world wars. The model illustrated has a parkerized blade as this was the pattern used before modification during World War II. Others with blued or bright blades saw service in World War I.

The finish of these bayonets is superior to those produced during the war. The walnut grips are corrugated to improve grip when used as a fighting knife. These bayonets used during the war were issued with plastic-reinforced cloth scabbards.

This example is an early model and has the date of manufacture 1906 stamped on the left blade flat below the ordnance bomb. The manufacturer's initials S A for Springfield Arsenal appear above the ordnance mark. The right blade flat has the letters U S above the serial number 78517.

Blade length: 16in
Overall length: 20·56in
Muzzle ring diameter: ·625in
Weight: 1·11lb
Rifle: ·30–06 M 1903 Springfield and Garand

This illustration is reproduced in scale with those on pages 62 and 63.

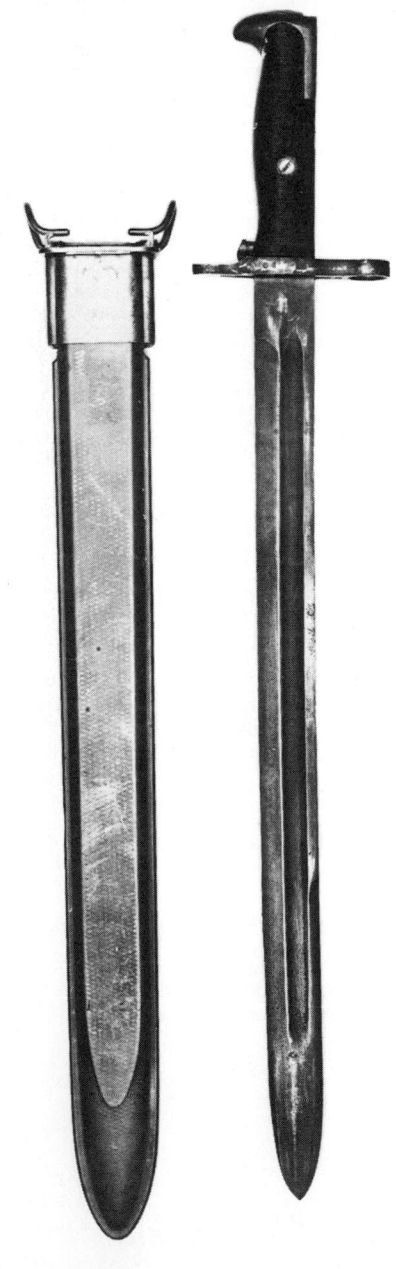

49. *Model 1942 Bayonet*

This bayonet is a modification of the Model 1905, which was the American infantryman's arm during the 1914–18 War. It can be recognised from the original design by the grips, which are made from plastic with a finely ribbed surface. These replaced the plain wood grips of the M 05 and proved far more appropriate to the damp and heat in the Pacific war.

An interesting feature of these bayonets is that the press stud is placed against the quillon and this operates the catch by a bar which pivots on the grip retaining screw. The catch is visible where it emerges as a hook in the lower part of the T-shaped pommel groove.

All metal parts were parkerised and the overall finish of these weapons is much poorer than the M 05s as speed of production was of prime importance. Their scabbards were made completely of an olive drab plastic-reinforced cloth which were easier to keep clean and free of mould and dust than those in use by the British.

The bayonet is marked on the left side of the blade with the manufacturer's stamp, the letters U.S. with between them the flaming bomb ordnance mark and the date, e.g. 1943. The scabbard is marked on the parkerised metal mouthpiece U.S. inside an ordnance bomb. Also there is a letter S stamped below this.

Blade length: 16in
Overall length: 20·56in
Muzzle ring diameter: ·625in
Weight: 1·11lb
Rifles: ·30–06 M 1903 Springfield
and Garand

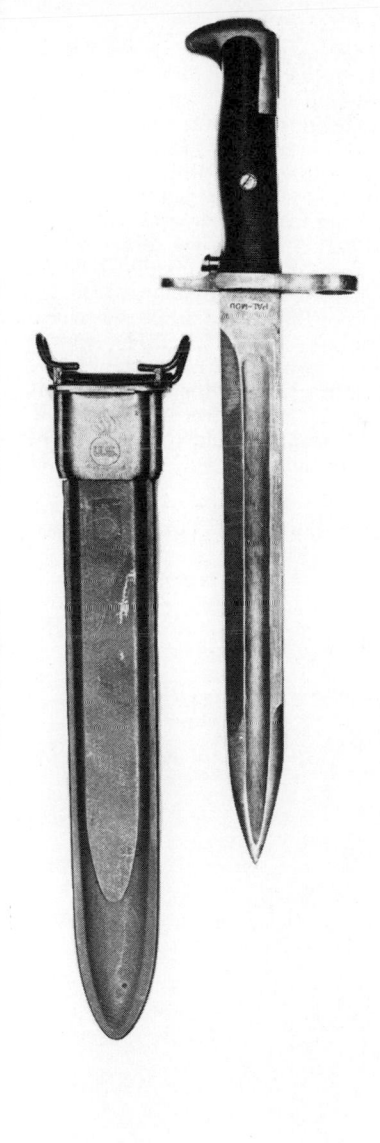

50. *Model 1905E1—Redesignated the M1, 1943*

In 1942 the U.S. Cavalry Board asked that the long M 1905 bayonet be shortened to make a more suitable arm for cavalry troops and for troops riding in vehicles. Consequently the last six inches were ground off the long models by the manufacturers and a short 10in bladed knife bayonet was produced. In spite of its initial designation the modification was carried out on the M 1942 so that examples of these bayonets have the markings and plastic grips of the World War II models. In March 1943 the M 1905E1 was finally approved, and was redesignated the M1. At the same time production of new short bayonets started and these too were M1 bayonets.

The example shown with the shortened blade, which is easily recognised as the fullers reach to the point, is parkerized on all metal surfaces of both blade and hilt. The grips are black but models can be found with grips varying from light brown to red. It is marked on the left side of the blade A.F.H., the manufacturer's initials, over U.S. with an ordnance bomb between the letters. Below these the date 1944 and on the right flat PAL-MOD to show that the conversion was carried out by PAL (MODification).

The scabbard shown is the M7 made by Victory Plastics and is stamped with their VP trademark on the plastic scabbard body below the parkerized steel mouthpiece. The letters US inside an ordnance bomb are stamped on the mouthpiece itself.

Blade length: 10in
Overall length: 14·56in
Muzzle ring diameter: ·625in
Weight: ·99lb
Rifle: M1 Garand and M 1903 Springfield

63

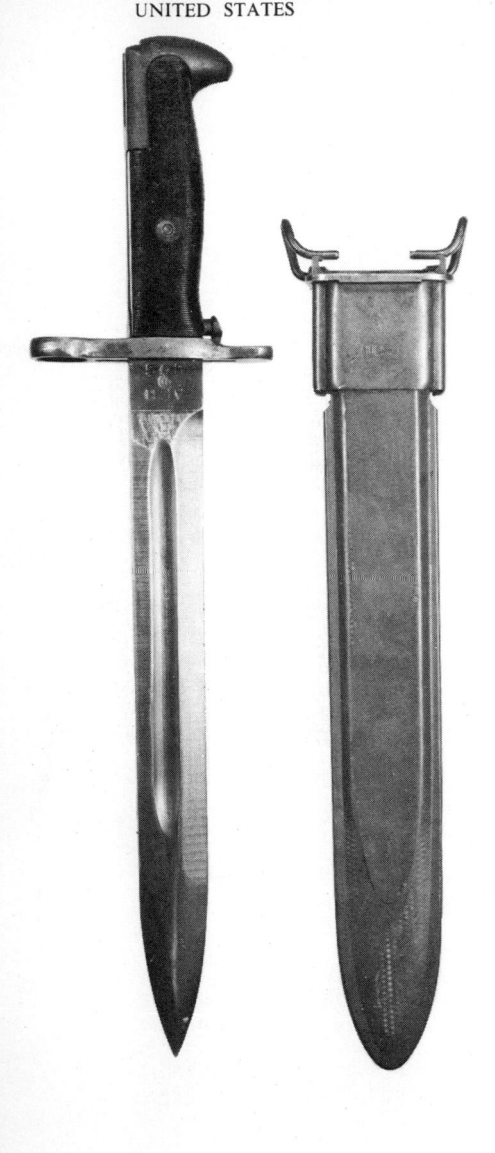

51. *M1 Bayonet*

This weapon was first made in March 1943 and it differs from the preceding model in that it is not a modification but was manufactured as a knife bayonet. The short blade has a fuller on either side which ends 3in from the point so distinguishing it from the modified M 1942s. In all other respects it is the same as the last model described.

There is no date stamped on the blade of this bayonet but the manufacturer's initials A.F.H. appear over the ordnance bomb flanked by the letters U.S. on the left side of the blade. All metal parts are parkerized.

The scabbard and the dimensions are the same for both types of M1 bayonet.

(Collection: Dr. John Kennaugh)

52. U.S. troops in training for D-Day. The M 1 Garand Rifle has the Model 1905 E 1 bayonet, later called M 1 bayonet (see plate 47).

65

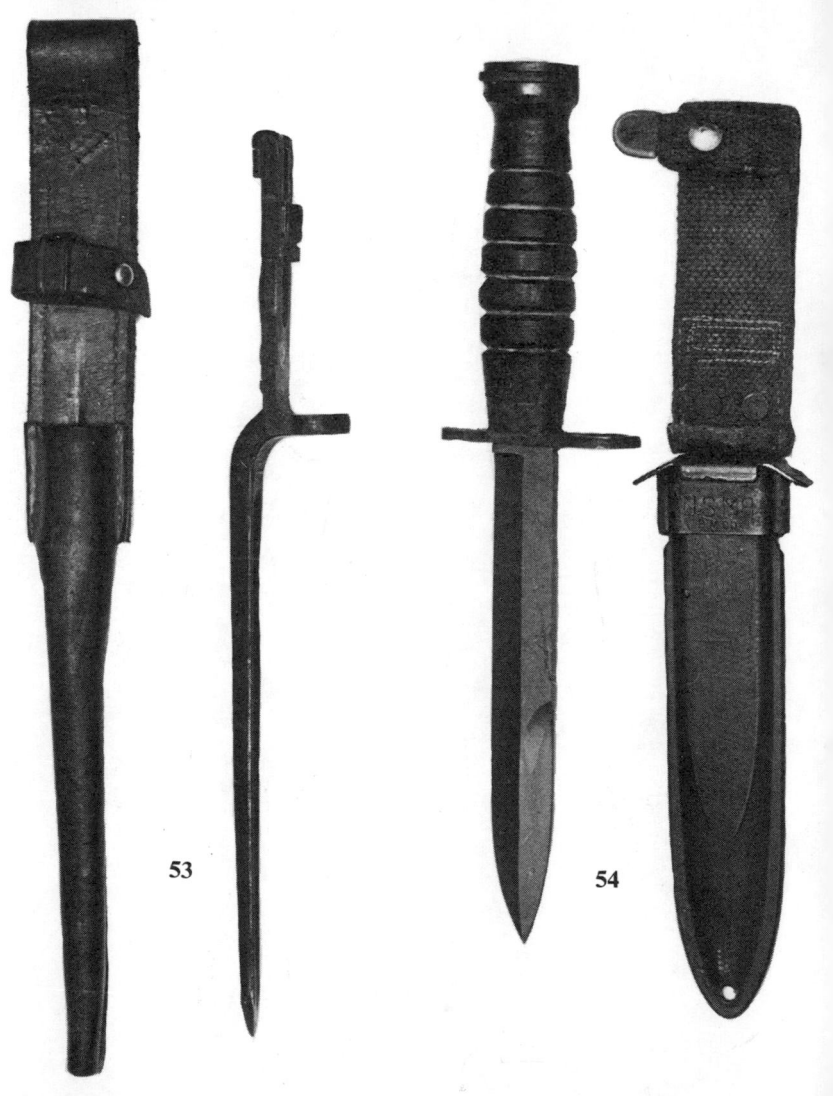

53

54

53. *Johnson Semi-Automatic Rifle Bayonet Model 1941*

This crude thrusting weapon, which resembles the ersatz bayonets produced by Austria at the end of the 1914–18 war, was issued in small numbers to the U.S. Marine Corps. However, it was issued in far greater numbers to Dutch forces, who also used the Johnson Semi-Automatic rifle.

Its design was greatly influenced by the recoiling barrel on the Johnson which could only operate with a light bayonet attached. The design was by Captain M. M. Johnson himself, but it was extremely unpopular with troops in action. It could only be used as a thrusting weapon and then only when attached to the rifle. It has no cutting edges and no real hilt: perhaps its design was partly justified since on a semi-automatic weapon the bayonet was intended for emergency use only.

The bayonet has a triangular fullered blade similar to those used on old socket bayonets. It is attached to the rifle by a muzzle ring and the flat blade tang has gaps cut out to accept a complicated attachment bar. This is held secure by a leaf spring held in place by a rivet.

The whole bayonet is parkerised and marked only by a serial number on the crossguard.

The scabbard is made entirely of leather and is stitched along the edges. The attached frog has a loop for a belt, but some have been seen that have had the American wire double hook slipped inside the belt loop. A serial number is stamped into the leather which may be either black or brown.

Blade length: 8in .
Overall length: 11·89in
Muzzle ring diameter: ·578in
Weight: ·34lb
Rifle: Johnson Semi-Automatic Rifle

54. *M4 Knife Bayonet*

In May 1944 the U.S. Infantry Board finally approved and designated the new bayonet the M4. This was the culmination of developments to find a bayonet for the M1 carbine, which had been approved in October 1941. The design accepted was an adaption of the M3 fighting knife, which had been carried by American forces in the Pacific arena together with their bayonet. The final version, the M4, was a close copy of the knife with modifications to enable it to be attached to the carbine. The modifications included a muzzle ring on the straight crossguard and an attachment groove with two pivoted press studs in the pommel.

The short single edged blade with a double edged point was ideal for its dual purpose role as bayonet and knife. Although the hilts have been altered since the war the present American bayonet, the M7, still utilises the same blade. The hilt was formed from rings of leather, which slipped over the tang and were compressed together by the pommel. The only serious fault found during the war in the Pacific was that the leather grips were prone to fungus and rot in the humid atmosphere. The worst point was close to the crossguard where the damp ran down. On many bayonets the last section of leather was removed and replaced by one of a resin compound. The model illustrated has been modified in this way. The original section flared out at the guard as at the pommel.

All metal parts of the bayonet were heavily parkerised. This particular bayonet is stamped on the forward face of the crossguard U.S. M4 above the manufacturer's name CASE. The American ordnance flaming bomb appears on the other side of the guard.

The scabbard illustrated is the M8, of which only 300,000 were made. The webbing frog is attached to the steel mouthpiece. The body is cloth reinforced by olive plastic made by Victory Plastics. The mouthpiece is marked U.S. M8 above B.M.CO. for Beckwith Manufacturing Company.

Those M4 bayonets with plastic grips were postwar developments and were equipped with the M8A1 scabbard.

Blade length: 6¾in
Overall length: 11·83in
Muzzle ring diameter: ·578in
Weight: ·56lb
Rifle: U.S. M1 Carbine

Other manufacturers: K1, PAL, CAMILLUS, UTICA, AERIAL, ACC, IMPERIAL.

A few M4 bayonets were manufactured and issued experimentally with moulded rubber grips. Very few of these were in action and they were soon abandoned by the Americans.

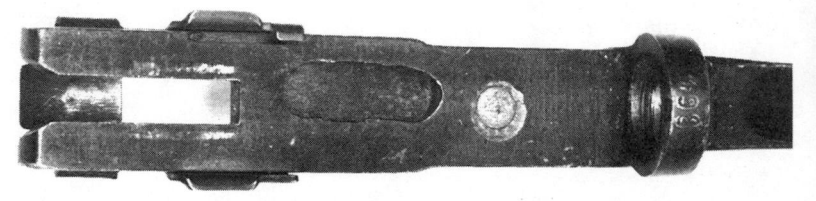

55. U.S.A. Johnson Semi-Automatic Rifle Bayonet Model 1941, hilt facing, showing details of hilt, spring and muzzle ring.

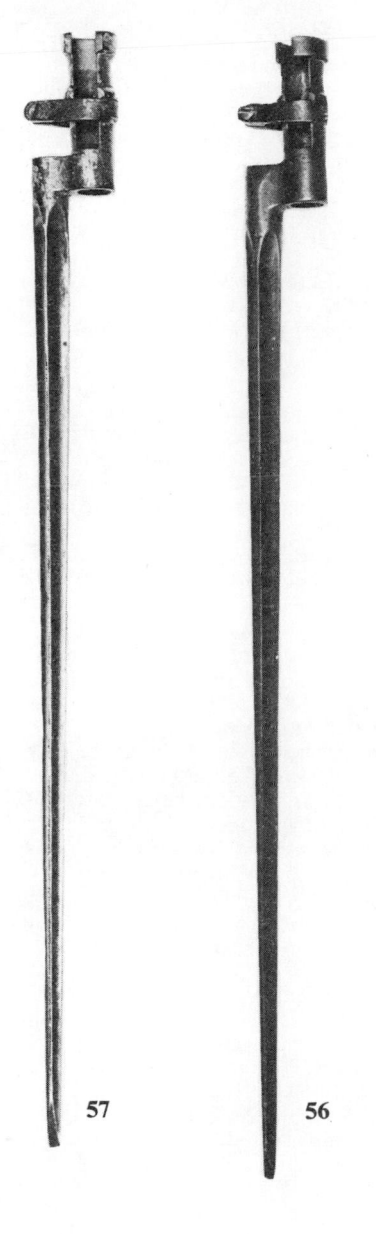

56. *Model 1891 Socket Bayonet*

In 1891 the Imperial Russian Army adopted the first of their Mosin-Nagant infantry rifles. With modifications these rifles have continued in use to the present day in Soviet satellite states. The Russian bayonet was intended to be a simple thrusting weapon and was carried attached to the rifle at all times: consequently no scabbards were provided for the infantry, although some cavalry troops armed with both sabre and rifle carried their bayonets in two mounts on the sword scabbard.

The Model 1891 socket bayonet has a long tapering cruciform blade ending in a screwdriver point. The socket itself, attached to the blade by a strong but extremely short elbow, has a locking ring form of attachment favoured by most countries in the mid-nineteenth century. The socket passes down the barrel and the foresight slides into the slot. The bayonet is twisted so that the foresight moves across the elbowed slot to the end. The locking ring when rotated locks the foresight in position thereby securing the weapon.

The whole bayonet has a dull parkerised finish and is stamped with the bow and arrow mark of the Tula arsenal. Two serial numbers are on the elbow. Small markings in the form of stars appear on the socket.

This pattern of bayonet saw considerable service in both world wars. Those found in metal scabbards are weapons that have been utilised by the Germans or Austrians after capture during the 1914–18 War.

Blade length: $16\frac{7}{8}$in
Overall length: $19\frac{5}{8}$in
Muzzle ring diameter: 15·5mm
Rifles: 7·62mm M 1891
    Mosin-Nagant Infantry Rifle
    Dragoon Rifle Model 1891

(Collection: David Jeffcoat)

57   56

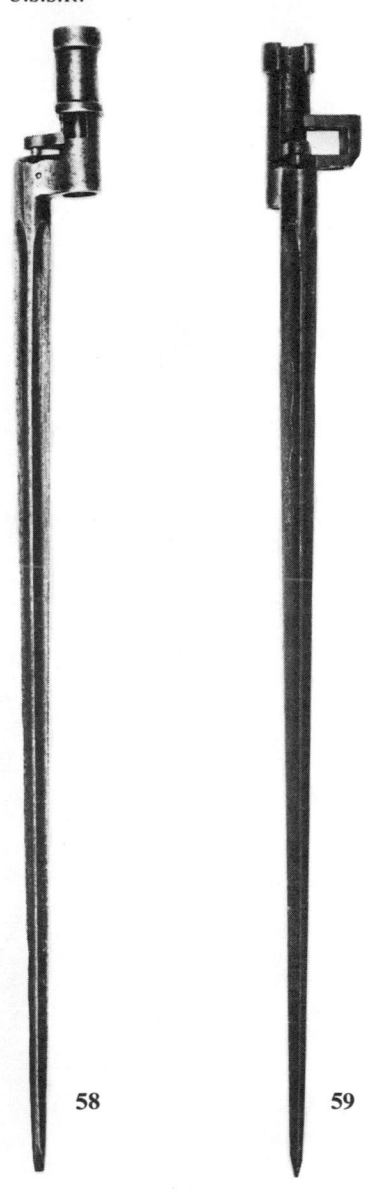

58

59

57. *Model 1891 Socket Bayonet.*

Variation: This bayonet, the first type to be manufactured, differs from the previous model described in that the socket slot is straight and all dimensions are slightly smaller.

Blade length: 16½in
Overall length: 19·19in

(Collection Kevin Bestt)

58. *Model 1891/30 Socket Bayonet*

This bayonet is identical to the preceding model except that the method of attachment to the rifle or carbine has been improved. The socket bayonet continued in production with the infantry rifle up to and during the 1940–45 war with Germany. This bayonet was first issued with the improved and modified Model 1891 rifle designated the Model 1891/30.

On this bayonet the locking ring has been rejected in favour of a press stud positioned in the elbow of the socket. This press stud with its knurled catch is held in position with a spring inside the elbow by a single rivet. The socket has an L-shaped mortice or slot. The barrel foresight passes down this and sideways so that the press stud simply blocks its exit, thereby locking it in position.

The whole bayonet is blued. A serial number and a small star are stamped on the socket elbow.

Blade length: 17in
Overall length: 19¾in
Muzzle ring diameter: 15·5mm
Rifles: 7·62mm Model 1891,
    Model 1891/30,
    Dragoon Model 1891 and the
    Sniper rifle Model 1891/30

59. *Model 1891/30 Socket Bayonet with foresight guard*

This bayonet is exactly the same as the previous Model 1891/30 except that a foresight guard or hood has been added to the socket. When this bayonet is fixed in position the foresight protrudes above the line of the socket so that the rifle may be aimed at all times. In order to protect the sight from damage this steel cover will stop a blow from any angle while its open ends allow free sighting. The two hood mounts are attached to the base on the socket by two dovetail joints; the cover may be slid off easily after removing a single screw through the joint closest to the blade.

The whole bayonet is heavily blued overall. It has the serial number 88507 stamped on the shank of the blade together with a small star.

All dimensions are the same as those of the Model 1891/30, but this weapon may only be used on the Model 1891 as later rifles were made with foresight guards on the barrel.

Not many were manufactured as it was found to be a difficult modification.

(Both from collection of David Jeffcoat)

60. Closeup of U.S.S.R. Model 1891/30 Socket Bayonet with foresight guard.

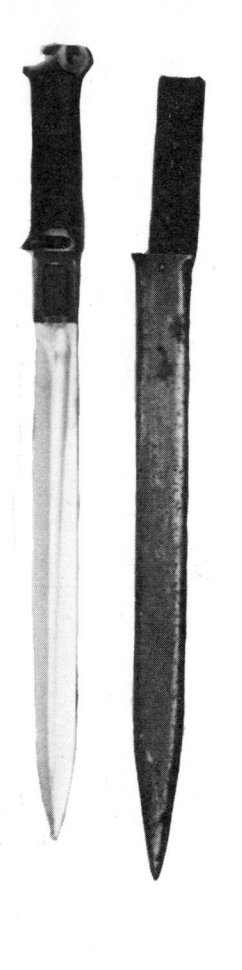

61. *Model 1936 Simonov Bayonet*

The Simonov Model 1936 (AVS) Automatic rifle was one of the first automatic rifles issued to the Soviet army, but it did not prove a success and has since been declared obsolete. It was however used throughout the World War II in limited quantities.

The long knife bayonet issued with this rifle has many unusual features. The double-edged blade has a longer fuller on the lower edge than on the back edge and the fullers which run close to the point are placed diagonally on the blade and taper towards the point. The right blade flat has the serial number 5754 stamped within a rectangular base lower than the rest of the blade. The wood grips, which are held in place by one screwbolt, have their central part chequered to improve the hand grip. The hilt also features a unique form of attachment mechanism. The pommel has a groove which slots onto a round bar, and this is positioned at right angles to the barrel. A sprung lever then clips this rigidly in position. At the same time a hook, placed closer to the rifle muzzle, enters a rectangular hole at the back of the hilt and holds the bayonet level with the barrel.

The scabbard is made entirely of steel and has a leather webbing frog riveted to two loops at the back.

This extremely complicated method of attachment was matched by the rifle's mechanism and led to its abandonment by a country which has always favoured simplicity in its small arms design.

Blade length: 13·06in (33·2cm)
Overall length: 18·3in (46·5cm)
Rifle: 7·62mm Model 1936 (AVS) Simonov Automatic Rifle

(Collection: Major a.D. Hans Rudolf von Stein)

72

62 and 63. *Model 1938 and Model 1940 Tokarev Bayonets*

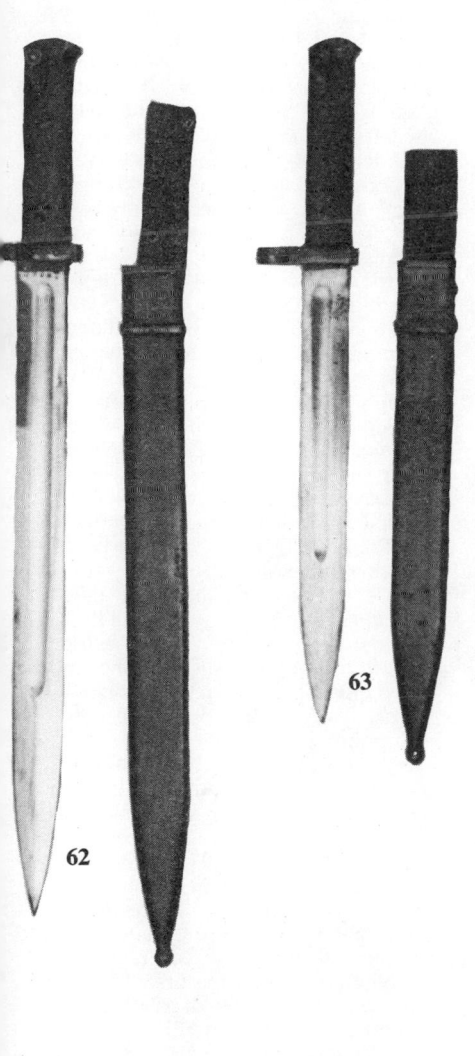

These two bayonets, though originally intended for two different rifles, are interchangeable and differ only in their blade lengths. The Model 1938 Tokarev semi-automatic rifle was lightly built with a two-piece stock and was issued with a conventional bayonet. It has a single-edged blade ending in a double-edged point. The fullers are placed slightly diagonally on the blade. The crossguard is held in place by two rivets, whose domed heads are visible. The plain wood grips are shaped to fit under the pommel. A conventional T-shaped groove and internal coiled spring press stud complete the attachment mechanism. The hilt is heavily blued, while the blade is polished bright.

The steel scabbard has a leather belt frog riveted to a loop on the back.

In 1940 a stronger version of the Tokarev semi-automatic rifle was introduced, but this still proved difficult to maintain under war conditions and these rifles have been abandoned by the U.S.S.R. since the war. The bayonet for this rifle is identical to the Model 1938 except that it has a short knife blade and a straight fuller. The rivets holding the crossguard are not visible on this model. The steel scabbard has a webbing frog.

These semi-automatic rifles were used throughout the Soviet army particularly by NCOs.

Model 1938
    Blade length: 14·25in
    Overall length: 19·69in
    Muzzle ring diameter: 14·5mm
    Rifle: 7·62mm Model 1938 (SVT)
      Tokarev Semi-Automatic Rifle

Model 1940
    Blade length: 9·62in
    Overall length: 15·19in
    Muzzle ring diameter: 14·5mm
    Rifle: 7·62mm Model 1940 (SVT)
      Tokarev Semi-Automatic Rifle

(Collection: Major a.D. Hans Rudolf von Stein)

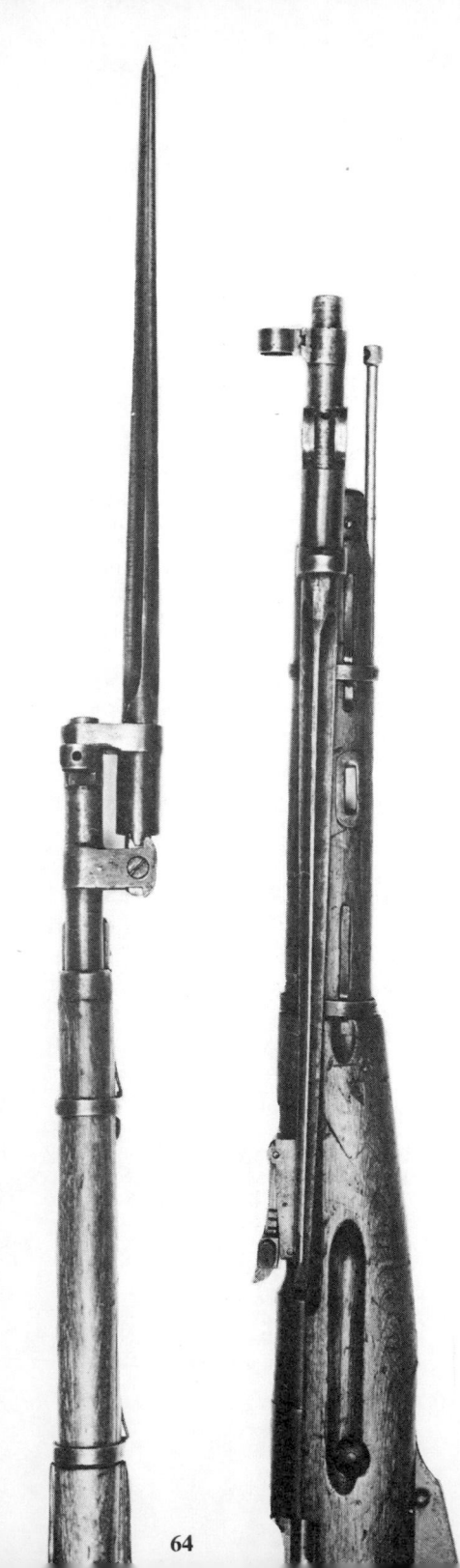

64 and **65.** *Model 1944*
Mosin-Nagant Carbine
Folding Bayonet

Towards the end of the war the Russian armies were equipped with the Model 1944 Carbine which was to be the last of the long line of Mosin-Nagants although it is still in use in some Soviet satellite states. It is basically the same carbine as the Model 1938 except that the barrel is slightly longer and it is equipped with a permanently attached folding bayonet. This then was a standard Soviet infantry weapon in the closing stages of the war leading up to the fall of Berlin in 1945.

This bayonet retains the blade form used on the first Mosin-Nagant having a straight cruciform blade with a screwdriver point. It may be folded or fixed in position by sliding the spring-loaded bayonet tube away from the pivot bolt and then swinging the bayonet to either position. When folded it lies alongside the stock, kept in place by a notch on the pivot, which engages the sprung tube. When attached an opposite catch combined with the muzzle ring holds it securely in position. This muzzle ring is part of the sliding tube and thus moves beyond the muzzle to spring back and stop against the foresight.

.As this bayonet is permanently attached to the carbine it was designed purely as a thrusting weapon since it could not be used separately in the hand.

The bayonet and carbine are heavily blued overall. There are no markings on the bayonet since it is an integral part of the carbine. The carbine bears the Tula arsenal mark on the receiver, the date 1945, the hammer and sickle within a wreath and the serial number Бг 4995.

Blade length: 12¼in
Overall length: 15⅛in
Muzzle ring diameter: 14·5mm
Rifle: 7·62mm M 1944 Carbine

(Collection: David Jeffcoat)

66. A Russian infantryman in Berlin, May 1945. He carries a Mosin–Nagant Model 1944 carbine.

75

APPENDIX 1

Comparative Lengths of Allied Bayonets

	Blade length		Overall length		Muzzle Ring diameters
Australia					
Pattern 1907	17in	(43·2cm)	21·75in	(55·3cm)	17mm
Pattern 1943 Machete	11·38in	(28·9cm)	16in	(40·6cm)	17mm
Pattern 1943 Owen	10·13in	(25·7cm)	14·9in	(37·8cm)	17mm
Pattern 1944	17in	(43·2cm)	21·75in	(55·3cm)	23mm
Belgium					
Model 1916	17·63in	(44·8cm)	22·38in	(56·9cm)	17·5mm
M 1916 Gendarmerie	17·63in	(44·8cm)	22·38in	(56·9cm)	17·5mm
Model 1924	17·63in	(44·8cm)	22·38in	(56·9cm)	15·5mm
M 1924 Shortened	13·18in	(33·5cm)	17·93in	(45·6cm)	15·5mm
Denmark					
M 1915	17·89in	(45·4cm)	22·08in	(56·1cm)	14mm
France					
Model 1886/93/16	20·5in	(52·0cm)	25·13in	(63·8cm)	22mm
Model 1886/93/16/35	13·25in	(33·7cm)	17·89in	(45·4cm)	22mm
M 1886/35	13in	(33·0cm)	17·63in	(44·8cm)	22mm
M 1892	15·75in	(40·0cm)	20·25in	(51·4cm)	13mm
M 1936 M.A.S.	13·25in	(33·7cm)	17in	(43·2cm)	—
Greece					
Model 1903	15·25in	(38·7cm)	19·63in	(49·9cm)	14mm
Model 1924	15·13in	(38·5cm)	20·25in	(51·4cm)	15·5mm
India					
Pattern Mk I*	12in	(30·5cm)	16·75in	(42·5cm)	17mm
Mk II and III	12in	(30·5cm)	16·75in	(42·5cm)	17mm
Netherlands					
M 1895 Infantry	14·13in	(35·9cm)	18·89in	(48·0cm)	14·5mm
M 1895 with quillon	14·13in	(35·9cm)	18·89in	(48·0cm)	14·5mm
M 1895 Cavalry	9·89in	(25·1cm)	14·63in	(37·2cm)	14·5mm
M 1895 Cavalry	9·89in	(25·1cm)	14·63in	(37·2cm)	14·5mm
M 1895 Carbine folding	12in	(30·5cm)	14·09in	(35·8cm)	—
M 1895 Artillery	19in	(48·3cm)	23·75in	(60·7cm)	14·5mm
M 1895 Marines	14·13in	(35·9cm)	18·89in	(48·0cm)	14·5mm

	Blade length		Overall length		Muzzle Ring diameters
Norway					
M 1894 Knife bayonet	8·38in	(21·3cm)	13·13in	(33·3cm)	—
M 1894	14·5in	(36·7cm)	19·25in	(48·9cm)	—
M 1894 Shortened	8·5in	(21·6cm)	13·25in	(33·7cm)	—
Poland					
M 1924 (1)	10in	(25·4cm)	15·2in	(38·6cm)	15·5mm
M 1924 (2)	10in	(25·4cm)	15·25in	(38·8cm)	—
United Kingdom					
Pattern 1907	17in	(43·2cm)	21·75in	(55·3cm)	17mm
Pattern 1917	17in	(43·2cm)	21·75in	(55·3cm)	15·5mm
No 4 Mk I	7·89in	(20·0cm)	9·89in	(25·1cm)	15·5mm
No 4 Mk II	7·89in	(20·0cm)	9·89in	(25·1cm)	15·5mm
No 4 Mk II*	7·89in	(20.0cm)	9·89in	(25·1cm)	15·5mm
No 4 Mk III	7·25in	(18·5cm)	9·89in	(25·1cm)	15·5mm
No 5 Mk I and II	8in	(20·4cm)	11·89in	(30·2cm)	23mm
United States					
Model 1905	16in	(40·6cm)	20·56in	(52·6cm)	16mm
Model 1942	16in	(40·6cm)	20·56in	(52·6cm)	16mm
M 42 shortened to					
M 1	10in	(25·4cm)	14·56in	(37·0cm)	16mm
M 1	10in	(25·4cm)	14·56in	(37·0cm)	16mm
Johnson	8in	(20·4cm)	11·89in	(30·2cm)	14·5mm
M4	6·75in	(17·2cm)	11·83in	(30·1cm)	14·75mm
U.S.S.R					
M 1891	16·89in	(42·9 cm)	19·63in	(49·9cm)	15·5mm
M 1891 Variation	16·5in	(41·9cm)	19·19in	(48·8cm)	15·5mm
M 1891/30	17in	(43·2cm)	19·75in	(50·2cm)	15·5mm
M 1891/30 with guard	17in	(43·2cm)	19·75in	(50·2cm)	15·5mm
M 1936 Simonov					
M 1938 Tokarev					
M 1940 Tokarev					
M 1944 Mosin-Nagant	12·25in	(31·2cm)	15·13in	(38·2cm)	14·5mm

— indicates no muzzle ring on bayonet

APPENDIX 2

Captured Bayonets

European armies have always sought to utilise captured material for their own troops. During the 1914–18 War German reserve troops were sometimes armed with French weapons of the 1860s originally taken during the Franco–Prussian War of 1870–71. The Germans have shown the greatest ingenuity in modifying captured arms including bayonets for their use but this practice was most prevalent during World War I. The modifications are usually obvious in that most of these bayonets were altered to fit Mauser rifles. They often have German regimental markings, are stamped with the Imperial German Eagle or marked "Deutschland" on the pommels. These are not difficult to catalogue but should be noted since many European armies continued to use arms in World War II which were first issued in World War I.

The Russian Model 1891 socket bayonet which was used during both wars can be found with scabbards, but these are World War I weapons. Those with straight tubular steel scabbards were used by the Austrians and those with tapering zinc scabbards by the Germans.

The 1939–45 war saw less use of captured weapons since the supply of small arms was usually adequate in comparison with the first war. Polish bayonets, which would fit the German Mausers without modification were reissued to the Wehrmacht, but these are heavily blued and often stamped with an eagle and a swastika.

French bayonets of the types used during World War II can be found stamped WZ 86 or WZ 92. The WZ is the Polish abbreviation for Model 1886 or 1892 and these weapons were carried by some Polish reserves.

While many bayonets especially French were carried by German reservists these are arms taken and modified during World War I and are strictly principal bayonets of that period. Other combatant nations did not follow this practice but the markings found on all bayonets are of prime importance in identification for a relatively common item may prove on closer inspection to be a rare requisitioned bayonet with a much more interesting history and a greater value to the collector. Particular care should be taken with British bayonets since these may have been issued to different nations in the Commonwealth.

APPENDIX 3

Collecting Bayonets

The majority of the bayonets described in this book can still be found without too much difficulty, and while bayonet values are rising year by year they are still the cheapest branch of arms collecting.

In spite of their obvious plainness and strength bayonets do need considerable care lavished upon them particularly if any restoration is needed. People have different ideas about how much any weapon may be restored without damaging it or lowering its value, but often these views are simply a matter of individual taste. The one important rule is that no restoration should destroy any of the original finish or, more important still, obliterate the markings. Some dealers tend to buff or highly polish weapons for sale to such an extent that a bayonet looks as if it has been plated. These are valueless to collectors and only suitable for decoration.

A power tool with a wire brush attachment can be used to remove surface rust, but care should be taken not to apply the brush too hard. Used carefully it will not in any way damage the bayonet but will avoid many hours of tedious work with emery paper. Where the original surface has been blued only wire wool of the finest grade should be used with a liberal use of oil, since this will remove any surface rust without damaging the blueing. Emery paper will damage parkerised blades since it will destroy the rough grained effect by polishing; again only wire wool should be used on this surface. Heavy rust can usually be scraped away, but a power tool will do this more easily again, providing care is taken, for sharp edges can easily be rounded by too much pressure. Finally a fine coating of oil or furniture polish will prevent further damage from a blade's worst enemy, fingerprints, which rust steel so badly. Lacquering gives a greater protection as does varnish but this often yellows and is difficult to remove.

Wood grips which are attached by bolts can be removed for cleaning providing a penetrating oil is used first so that the bolts will not damage the wood when removed. Most bayonets have the grips attached by round bolt heads which are cut across and can be removed if a normal screwdriver is cut and filed to remove the centre which would be blocked by the threaded bolt. These are best scrubbed, allowed to dry thoroughly and treated with a good

79

furniture polish like Antiquax. Leather scabbards are sometimes brittle but can be preserved by using a saddle soap followed by liberal use of shoe polish.

Re-blueing is attempted by some collectors but it should be remembered that the majority of collectors do not do this and, further, will not value any weapon restored to this extent. Repainting scabbards which were once camouflaged does not on the other hand do anything but protect the bayonet from rust and can always be removed.

Some record should be taken of a bayonet's details before it is displayed since records of markings especially are of invaluable use in identifying rarer models. Some collectors prefer to keep their collections in drawers away from dust and interference, but if a display is desirable, pegboard is certainly the best method since it allows the bayonets to be removed or changed in position easily as well as offering a fairly cheap way of mounting a collection.

Fortunately, bayonets are not yet of sufficient value to attract the faker, nor are parts often replaced since it is far simpler to find a good example. If investment is an important factor bayonets should only be acquired, where possible, if complete with scabbard and belt frog. Though the belt frogs are of little value in themselves they do complete the arm. The serial numbers on bayonet and scabbard very rarely tally so if a scabbard is found later it may fairly be added to the bayonet.

Finally, bayonets with other military arms have one distinct advantage to the collector in that complete sets or collections may be built. Each one is a step in a country's arms development. Once the bayonet is acquired by buying or exchanging the interest really starts by looking into its history, especially if it has regimental markings, and I hope this book may help solve many problems in this field of research.

Select Bibliography

Carter, J. Anthony. "Bayonets". A continuing series, commencing October 1965. *Guns Review*, London.

Hardin, Albert N., Jr. *The American Bayonet, 1776–1964*. Pennsylvania, 1964.

Hicks, Major James E. *French Military Weapons, 1717–1938*. Connecticut, 1964.

Nielsen, O., and Skaar, F. C. *Haerens Handvapen*. Oslo.

Reynolds, Major E. G. B. *The Lee-Enfield Rifle*. London and New York, 1960.

Smith, W. H. B., and Joseph, E. *Small Arms of the World*. Pennsylvania, 1962.

Wilkinson-Latham, R. J. *British Military Bayonets, 1700 to 1945*. London and New York, 1967 and 1968.